Rory McIlroy: The Inspiring Story of One of Golf's Fearless Champions

An Unauthorized Biography

By: Clayton Geoffreys

Table of Contents

Foreword

Rory McIlroy made his professional debut in 2007 and wasted little time announcing himself to the world. By 2011, he won the U.S. Open, and within a few short years added both the PGA Championship and Open Championship in 2014. His accolades only grew from there: The Players Championship in 2019 and again in 2025, plus a groundbreaking moment in 2022 when he became the first golfer ever to capture the FedEx Cup three times.

Now 36, McIlroy remains a central figure in golf. With time still on his side, McIlroy isn't finished, he's still chasing majors and proving that his best game may yet be ahead of him. Thank you for purchasing *Rory McIlroy: The Inspiring Story of One of Golf's Fearless Champions*. In this unauthorized biography, we will learn Rory McIlroy's incredible life story and impact on the game of golf. Hope you enjoy and if you do, please do not forget to leave a review!

Also, check out my author website to join my exclusive list where I let you know about my latest books and so I can thank you for your purchase.

Cheers,

Clayton Geoffreys

Visit me at www.claytongeoffreys.com

Introduction

On August 10, 2011, Rory McIlroy put his first tee into the ground at Augusta National with a four-shot lead as he sought to become the second-youngest Masters champion in the game's history. He was already being hyped as golf's next big superstar, and everyone was anticipating him to steamroll the competition just like a 21-year-old Tiger Woods did 14 years earlier. The question was not whether McIlroy would win; it was by how *much*. Would it be a 12-shot runaway like Tiger in '97?

But 81 strokes later, McIlroy walked off the green with complete dejection on his face. It was a meltdown of epic proportions that Sunday, with shots sprayed all over the course and short putt after short putt sliding away. At one point on the 13th tee, after his tee ball went into the water and McIlroy realized the cause was lost, his head sank into his arms in despair. The world could feel the pain he was experiencing just by looking at his face.

The media wrote McIlroy off, thinking there was no way he could recover from this anytime soon. This would be a hard pill to swallow. But just two months later, McIlroy went to Congressional Country Club in Bethesda, Maryland, and put on a Tiger Woods-like show, building an eight-shot lead by Saturday afternoon and never letting anybody get closer. He would officially put that Masters debacle behind him as he, at the time, set the all-time U.S. Open scoring record in relation to par at -16. It was pure domination.

That was the beginning of a major championship run for Rory, who went on to win two PGA Championships and an Open Championship after that U.S. Open triumph. However, despite constantly being recognized as one of the top players in the world, one thing was still missing: a green jacket.

Year after year, McIlroy went to Augusta National seeking a Masters title, and he kept coming up empty. It was the only major he had not won. To put it in perspective, only six golfers in the game's treasured history have won all four major championships: Jack Nicklaus, Tiger Woods, Gary Player, Walter Hagen, Gene Sarazen, and Ben Hogan. They are all the greatest legends of the game, but Rory was struggling to join that group, and it looked like it would never happen. The weight on his shoulders kept piling up as the media continued to grill him about why he could not win that elusive tournament. McIlroy wanted to win it so badly, but he just could not do it.

He even started to believe that it was never going to happen—that was, until April 13, 2025, when McIlroy stormed to the top of the leaderboard in the third round and then built a commanding lead on Sunday with just six holes to play. He finally appeared to have that elusive green jacket in sight. But another collapse looked imminent when he dunked an easy wedge into the water on the 13th hole. Then, after another slip-up on 14, he fell out of first place behind Justin Rose.

McIlroy rallied with a heroic shot on 15 and a birdie on 17, thus sending him to the 18th hole with a one-shot lead. But once again, he squandered it away and would go to a playoff with Rose. Everybody watching could feel the tension, as McIlroy knew it was now or never when it came to the Masters. Indeed, he might never get this close again. It was a life-turning moment for him—it was either going to go one way or the other.

Then, from the middle of the 18th fairway in the playoff with Rose, McIlroy hit an iron shot for the ages, one that fed down to the slope and stopped just a few feet from the cup. After Rose missed his birdie, McIlroy knocked his short putt in only to fall to the ground in exhaustion and jubilation. He broke down in tears. He had done it!

It was a release of so much pressure, and he let it all out. He was overcome with joy, unlike anybody else before him on that famous 18th green. He had accomplished his dream, something he had long been trying for and had put in so many hours of work for. McIlroy was now a career grand slam winner, and thus, had done something that not even Arnold Palmer, Tom Watson, or Phil Mickelson were able to do.

In many ways, Rory McIlroy's professional career has been very much like that final round of the Masters. It has been a lifetime of twists and turns with all kinds of drama and suspense along the way.

He was a teenage sensation who was seen as the Tiger Woods of Europe as a young boy, and he began his career living up to those lofty expectations with apparent ease, having won four major championships by the age of 25. But then, things went sideways for a while, as Rory went more than 10 years without winning a major. He fought his swing;

he fought his putting; and perhaps the most daunting challenge of all, Rory fought his inner demons, even as the media's dogged attentions made those demons appear bigger.

For every high moment Rory has had, like the career grand slam, three FedEx Cup titles, and Ryder Cup glory, there were bad memories, too. Like the 2011 Masters and, more recently, the 2024 U.S. Open, wherein he missed two short putts over the final three holes to essentially throw away the trophy. Or the 2022 Open Championship at St. Andrew's, where he just could not make a putt and watched his back-nine lead slip away. Make no mistake about it—not many golfers have fought back from adversity like Rory has. He is as mentally strong a player as there ever has been. He is also one of the most talented to ever pick a club.

McIlroy grew up in Northern Ireland, the only son of two devoted parents who sacrificed a great deal to give him a chance at living his dream. His father, Gerry, once said he did not have the greatest skills in the world when it came to work, but he would do whatever it took to get his son the money he needed to play golf and get better at it.

"I'll never be able to repay Mum and Dad for what they did, but at least they know they'll never have to work another day. I'll do whatever it takes to look after them," McIlroy said of his parents' sacrifices.[i]

When McIlroy was just 15 years old, he won his first-ever junior golf tournament. He only flourished from there, and his name grew as he quickly became famous in Ireland as a future star. Much like Tiger

Woods, he appeared on television shows as a young boy and showcased his skills. And from there, the hype only continued to spread.

"If the Americans have Tiger Woods, we have young Rory," famous golfer and Northern Irishman Darren Clarke said, a former Open champion himself.

Not many people in America knew who Rory McIlroy was, though, until he made his major championship debut at the 2007 Open Championship at Carnoustie as an 18-year-old amateur. He had qualified by winning the European Amateur Championship in 2006. That opening round at Carnoustie, "The Kid," as the announcers called him, threw darts at the hole live on American television, leaving everyone in awe.

"This kid's going to be something one day," were the words of TNT analyst Bobby Clampett.[ii]

McIlroy shot a 68, tying him for third place after the first round. He went on to win the Low Amateur title, recognized as the Silver Medal, as he introduced himself to the world. Three years later at St. Andrew's, he tied the major championship record with a first-round 63 at the Open.

McIlroy's resume is Hall-of-Fame worthy already. Along with his five major championships, McIlroy has won 29 times on the PGA Tour and 19 times on the European (DP World) Tour. He is the current No. 2-ranked golfer in the world, behind only Scottie Scheffler. He has three FedEx Cup titles, six Race to Dubai titles, has been named PGA Tour

Player of the Year three times, and European Tour Player of the Year four times. And he is only 36 years old![iii]

McIlroy is one of just 25 men to reach the top as No. 1 in the world. He has been there on nine separate occasions, the most recent being in 2022. Overall, he has spent 122 weeks as the world's No. 1, the fifth-most of any player in golf. Most expect McIlroy to be No. 1 again, but he will have to catch Scottie Scheffler to do so.[iv]

Meanwhile, McIlroy has achieved just as much success off the course, getting himself involved in numerous prosperous business ventures. Tiger Woods and McIlroy recently launched the TGL Golf League, an indoor team league using simulators for the competition. Airing on ESPN, it was a massive success and is set to return in 2026. He also has a $20 million deal with Nike and has his own business in Rory McIlroy Management Services Ltd. All in all, McIlroy's off-course business income is set annually at $32 million.

McIlroy is also one of the most giving athletes on the PGA Tour. After winning the 2025 Players Championship, he donated his entire $4.5 million in earnings to Mencap Charity, an organization that raises awareness for those with Down syndrome back home in Northern Ireland. McIlroy donated a lot of his Masters winnings toward the charity as well. It is all part of the goal of the Rory McIlroy Foundation, which is to support children's charities all across the world.

Rory McIlroy is one of the most respected golfers on the PGA Tour, and his success has been great for the game, inspiring new players and attracting legions of new fans in the modern age. Now, with the career grand slam behind him, McIlroy still has much to look forward to. Along with possibly winning more major championships and Ryder Cup titles, he will undoubtedly continue to build his growing legacy as one of the most intriguing golfers of our time.

Chapter 1: Early Childhood

Rory McIlroy was born on May 4, 1989, in Holywood, County Down, Northern Ireland, to Gerry McIlroy and Rosie McDonald. Rory spent most of his early life there, starting at St. Patrick's School, a Catholic school, in the County Down area just south of Belfast. His headmaster, Martin Meyler, described him as very laid-back and someone who was never affected by anything.

Rory's parents, Gerry and Rosie, worked extremely hard to give Rory, their only child, the best life possible. Rosie worked the night shift at the 3M factory, many times cooking dinner early and leaving it for Rory and Gerry when they got home. Gerry, meanwhile, worked almost the opposite hours of Rosie, from noon until midnight, as both a bartender and sports club associate.

"They basically never saw each other. We didn't take a family holiday for over a decade," Rory said.[i]

Gerry's work as a bartender at the Holywood Golf Club opened the door for his son to play golf when he got done with school and on the weekends. Rory developed a love for the game at such a young age because of his father, who was a scratch golfer. He would play regularly at Holywood and brought Rory along with him many times. Rory could be seen at just 10 months old crawling around the golf tee with a golf club in his tiny hand.

By the time he was two years old, he already had his own plastic set of clubs and was whacking at the ball better than a teenager could. Indeed, he was hitting it so well that he kept breaking the plastic clubs, leading Gerry to have to cut regular clubs down so they were proper for a young boy of his size; club providers do not create sets for toddlers!

The McIlroys were not poor, but they were not financially blessed, either. Both of Rory's parents had to work around the clock to give him a good life and make enough money to afford what he needed to fulfill his passion, which, to no one's surprise, would turn out to be golf. At just two years old, little Rory was hitting 40-yard drives that amazed people at Gerry's local golf club.

Gerry coached little Rory, who begged his father from the day he could talk to take him to Holywood Golf Club. Once Gerry taught Rory how to grip a club properly, Rory would take it to bed with him and sleep with his hands wrapped around it. And this was no temporary fixation, as his obsession only grew stronger as the years went by. By the time Rory was seven, Gerry asked his golf club to change their rules and allow his son to be admitted as a member, despite not being of proper age. The club agreed to Gerry's request and, thus, Rory was officially a member.

Videos soon emerged showing just how good this young boy was. The Irish public marveled at the child prodigy who was chipping balls into a washing machine and ripping drives down the fairway with his small clubs. When Rory was not playing, he was watching Nick Faldo on television, learning the ways to better himself.

Of course, Gerry wanted his son to be great, but he never pushed him. He let Rory discover his love for the game himself and always gave him the freedom to choose his career path. It is refreshing to see, given that so many parents force sports upon their children, and it sometimes ruins their passion for the game.

"I was never pushed into it in any way," Rory said. "If anything, it was the other way around. I had to drag my dad out to the golf course, so I was never pushed into playing golf. It was always my ambition, my dream, I had to drag my dad out to the golf course to play, so it was pure, pure joy and pure passion for me."[v]

The area where Rory grew up was a very tight-knit community. It resembled a small town where everybody knew each other and loved golf. So, Rory's fame in the area spread pretty quickly before he turned 10 years old.

"My hometown, Holywood, Northern Ireland, is a picturesque little coastal town with very welcoming people, superb restaurants, and homely pubs," Rory said about where he grew up.[v]

After Gerry taught Rory to master the basics, he handed over most of the coaching duties to Holywood golf pro Michael Bannon, who would be Rory's first true coach and mentor. Bannon formed a great relationship with the McIlroy family, working around their schedule so that he could coach Rory up into an eventual champion.

"He got good parents, and his parents were great," Bannon said. "They brought him up well, gave him the confidence, and you know, not to talk about myself, but maybe I was the right person in the right place at the time. I was lucky, too. And it's just a combination. I don't really know."[vi]

Bannon worked with Gerry, and one of the things they came up with when Rory was small was adjusting the pars on the golf course to improve his confidence. They would set a long par 4 as a par 6 or 7, and then eventually lower it as he got better. Rory would finish nine holes feeling like he shot under par, giving him a sense of accomplishment. It was a similar strategy that Earl Woods used with his son Tiger when he was little.

"It was really a smart thing because it gave him the confidence thinking, 'Yes, great, I was under par today," Bannon said. "Under par from the course that his dad had set up for him. So that's a good thing ... not to be afraid to be under par."[vi]

Being an only child, Rory was extremely close to his parents. At first, it was frustrating for him because he never saw them in the same house at the same time; one was always working. It took him a while to really appreciate what they were doing for him. Rosie and Gerry were doing all they could so he could advance his career in golf.

"The pride that they feel when I do well, I can feel that and I can sense that," Rory said. "When you're 10 or 11 or 12 years old, you don't realize the sacrifices that they're making for you. But once you get older, and you know a bit more about the world, you realize how much sacrifice they made for you."[i]

By the time Rory was 11, he was down to a 3 handicap, meaning he was averaging just a few strokes over par on a championship course. The progress he was making kept him going to the golf course.

Rory's parents taught him well—not just in golf, but in life. He was raised as a Catholic and went to a strict school that helped him develop a respect for elders. He was humble and had good grades, a trait that he says came from his parents. He called himself blessed as a young boy to have forged such a great relationship with both Rosie and Gerry.

"I couldn't ask to have two better parents," Rory said. "They're there for me at the worst of times, like this time last year after missing the cut, or the best of times, walking off as the champion golfer of the year. I can't speak highly enough of them. They're the best people in the world."[v]

Chapter 2: Junior/High School Career

By the time Rory was nine years old, he was on the junior circuit playing with the best young golfers in the world. He played in the U10 (Under 10) World Championship event at the Doral Country Club in Miami, Florida, where he got a hole-in-one. Rory would go on to win the event, establishing himself as the best golfer under 10 years old in the world.

He then appeared on a television show with Gerry Kelly and famous Northern Irish golfer Darren Clarke, who had predicted that Rory would be the next Tiger Woods.

It is not uncommon for youngsters to get tired of golf by the time they become teenagers. That could have been the fate for Rory as well, given how much time he was spending on the course. But a couple of things kept him interested.

First of all, he had a positive attitude. He did not let the frustrating aspects of the game get to him. Instead, he went about with a smile on his face and just had fun out there.

"Having fun is the most important aspect, and I have to sometimes tell myself that. Why did I start to play this game? Why did I start to play golf? It's because I loved it; because I have fun at it," Rory said later in life about his early golf days when giving advice to young golfers. "Junior golfers have to remember that—they have to remember to have fun. I'm trying to better myself by making birdies; making birdies is fun. That's my fun on the golf course."[vii]

Another thing Rory did was to limit how much time he spent on the driving range. The best way to really practice your game is to play actual rounds of golf. Playing around the course allowed him to learn how to hit creative shots and get better visuals of the course. It also helped him improve his short game. Michael Bannon would take him out every day and play a round, and Rory just constantly got better.

Perhaps the hardest part for Rory was getting him committed to school because he was so in love with golf. When Rory became a teenager, he moved to Sullivan Upper School, which was basically a high school in Northern Ireland. But McIlroy, who was famous by his teenage years for his golf game, sometimes missed school to play a round. The principal at Sullivan Upper, John Stevenson, did Rory a favor and excused him from classes so he could continue to pursue his dream.

"Sometimes you've got to break a few rules," Stevenson said.[viii]

Stevenson sent a memo to the teachers explaining Rory's absences and asked his teachers to supply work for him so he could get caught up at home. It was a risk the principal was taking, but he knew it would be worth it in the end.

"At the time, we wanted to look forward in anticipation to his future sporting success and recognize that we will have played some part in that," Stevenson said.[viii]

As time progressed, it was just getting harder for McIlroy to focus on school as he was traveling abroad playing junior golf tournaments. He even made the European Junior Ryder Cup team at just 15 years old, forcing Stevenson to send another memo out to teachers that McIlroy would miss time to compete.

The absences were getting excessive, though, as Rory continued to progress in golf. Gerry had a meeting with Stevenson and asked if Rory could miss extended time. At first, Stevenson put his foot down and said that Rory had to be in school. But eventually, he gave in to Gerry's request.

"I took a decision that if his parents had made these sacrifices and had done all this work on his behalf, that his school needed to do that too," Stevenson said. "When families, schools, and peer groups work well together, 'dreams are possible.' We were taking a risk; it could have fallen apart."

But by the time he was 16, Rory's high school days officially came to an end to focus on his amateur and eventual professional golf career. Given his talent, it was just something he could not pass up.

He was now officially an amateur and on his way to big things.

Chapter 3: Amateur Golf Career

After putting school aside, Rory McIlroy was now an amateur golfer competing with the world's other top players at that level. He had a stellar season in 2005, starting with amateur victories at the West of Ireland Championship and Irish Closed Championship.

However, McIlroy's first big splash as an amateur came at the 2005 North of Ireland Championship at Royal Portrush in Northern Ireland, which has hosted multiple Open Championships, including Shane Lowry's triumphant run in 2019. McIlroy was just 16 years old but looked every bit the part in terms of style. He showcased flash with a light pink mock turtleneck and a white-as-snow pair of pants that included a shiny pink belt.

"The confidence I had, and the cockiness I had at 16, sometimes I think I have to rediscover that a little bit," McIlroy said of his amateur career.[ix]

Unlike the short hair he has today, McIlroy was known for his long curly locks with blonde streaks as a teenager. He would take Royal Portrush by storm that day and become an even bigger rising star around the world.

The course record at Royal Portrush was a 65 set by three-time major champion Padraig Harrington. But McIlroy was going after it at just 16. It did not look like a special round after he missed a short birdie putt on the first hole, but just one hole later, McIlroy struck a six-iron onto the par-5 green and made a birdie. From there, it was an assault on the record books. His length was shocking as he was hitting wedges into par-5s. He shot a 33 on the front nine before really attacking pins on the backside.

McIlroy sank his eagle putt on the 10th and added another birdie on 11. He was now on pace to break Harrington's record, let alone win the championship. People were so in awe that even Michael Bannon was in shock when he got word, and Royal Portrush golf pro Gary McNeill shrugged it off as a joke when he got an update that McIlroy was about to break the course record.

"No one can shoot 61 around Royal Portrush," McNeill said.

McIlroy was 6-under on the round when he reached the 14th hole. But he then went on a birdie run just as the crowd gathered to watch history. The infamously long par-3 16th hole, known as Calamity Corner, would surely trip McIlroy up; however, he struck a shot close there and made a 2. He made birdies on 17 and 18 to close with five straight birdies and a course record 61, shattering Harrington's mark.

"Whenever I think about Royal Portrush and about links golf and my development, I always think about that round of golf," McIlroy said. "There are not many golf rounds where I remember every shot, but for that round, I do."[ix]

The excitement over McIlroy was now reaching fever pitch after that round of golf, which made headlines all across Northern Ireland. The hype was real around the kid as he climbed up the charts in the amateur world golf rankings, hoping to one day make it to No. 1 before he turned pro.

"There was always a feeling in Northern Ireland that we had a very big talent in Holywood, but it was only from age 12, 13, or 14 that we really started to hear about him," BBC reporter Stephen Watson said. "He started to break record after record after record, was on TV now and again, and so that was how we first heard of him."[ix]

The news reached across the Irish Sea, where the Open Championship that year was being held at St. Andrew's, Scotland. When Darren Clarke walked off the 18th green, he was immediately asked, not about his round but about the young teenage sensation who broke the course record. Another Northern Irishman, Graeme McDowell, commented on the news.

"You hear about the next great thing. 'We've got this kid, he's playing at plus-7 (handicap) and blah, blah, blah,'" McDowell said. "Then he shot 61 in the first round of qualifying for the North of Ireland, and I'm like, 'Really? OK. Hold on. Now I have to pay a little more attention to this.' That was probably the first time that I realized we had something pretty special on our hands."

That week at St. Andrew's, though, the man that McIlroy hoped to one day emulate was dominating the championship. McIlroy watched from home as Tiger Woods decimated the field for the second time at the Old Course to win the Claret Jug and Open Championship. It only fueled young McIlroy to play harder as he strived to achieve what Woods was doing so often.

McIlroy entered the Irish Amateur Open and found himself out of position after three days. But in the final round, he posted a 67 to shoot up the leaderboard and finish in fifth place.

Rory had high dreams as an amateur. With his career taking off and him rising up the world amateur rankings, he was ambitious in what he wanted out of his career.

"I want to win majors, play in Ryder Cups, and win Orders of Merit," he said. "All of that. There is no point in saying I want to be a journeyman. I don't want to finish top 60 in the Order of Merit every year. I want to go out and win, play the best I can, and go on from there. Obviously, you need to get into the top 50 in the world to play in majors, and I hope to do that after the first three or four years."[x]

McIlroy continued his rise in the amateur world in 2006. He successfully defended his titles at the West of Ireland Championships and Irish Amateur Close, becoming the first Irish golfer to go back-to-back. His success got him invitations to European Tour events, including the Dubai Desert Classic, where he got the chance to meet his idol, Tiger Woods. McIlroy shot back-to-back rounds of 72 there and missed the cut.

A 17-year-old McIlroy competed in his biggest amateur event yet in Milan, Italy, at the European Amateur Championships. The winner of the event would earn an invitation to the 2007 Open Championship. There, McIlroy dominated the competition, cruising to a three-shot victory. He admitted afterward how the opportunity to play in the Open Championship gave him extra motivation. The win also moved him to No. 1 in the world amateur rankings.

As 2007 progressed, the buildup around McIlroy continued. His mentors continued to praise him and warn the rest of the golf world that Europe's version of Tiger Woods was well on his way.

"You could see the raw talent he had all through the foundation time," Darren Clarke said, who mentored Rory when he was 13. "He was destined to be a top-class golfer. You see people in all walks of life with outstanding talent, in whatever arena, and he was in that category. He was way above what I had seen."[xi]

Rory's First Major

McIlroy's victory at the European Amateur Championship earned him a spot in the 2007 Open Championship at Carnoustie, Scotland, his first-ever major championship appearance. Outside of Europe, not many knew about him yet. America was still in love with Tiger Woods at the time, who was the defending champion at the Open Championship. However, those in Europe were very well aware of him, as were the executives of the Royal & Ancient, the committee that ran the Open Championship.

"Rory was the up-and-coming, swashbuckling amateur with a great career ahead of him," R&A chairman Peter Dawson said. "There was no doubt about that. He was recognized as the most likely lad to rise to stardom, but you can never be sure about these things. Many have looked good but never made it. He was known to us before the Open because of his amateur record. He was a very exciting young man, a real prodigy. Every year, there are good amateurs who come through, but very few of them have star quality. He clearly had star quality. He had a swagger, and he was good enough."[xi]

Rory McIlroy, now 18 years of age, was paired in the first two rounds with Miguel Angel Jimenez and Henrik Stenson, two European Ryder Cup players. It was anything but warm that day, as Rory strode to the tee in a black fleece top with a black hat over his long black locks. As he turned onto the back nine, McIlroy was -1 before striking an iron close on 12. After his birdie there, he put another one close on 13. McIlroy was -3 and just one back of Paul McGinley as American television began introducing their audience to him.

McIlroy would open with a first-round 68, one better than his idol, Tiger Woods. Sergio Garcia surged to the top of the leaderboard at the end of the day and shot 65 to take the lead into Friday. The story of the day, though, was McIlroy, who was greeted with a standing ovation by the Scottish crowd as he walked up to the 18th hole.

"It was just like a chill down the back of my spine with the ovation I got. I soaked up the atmosphere and really enjoyed it. I just wanted to come here, try to make the cut and win the Silver Medal [for the best amateur], and that was about it, really. I come into these weeks just trying to learn as much as possible. I think I'll be able to sleep all right. I'm knackered. It's a pretty special feeling to say you shot one better than Tiger."[xi]

McIlroy's second day was not as special, however, as the challenging course got the best of him. He went around in 76, but even at +2, it was good enough to make the cut and be around for the weekend. Being the only amateur to make the cut, he was assured of the Silver Medal.

McIlroy never contended over the weekend, but he still made an impression. In brutally difficult conditions on Saturday, he went around in 73.

"I watched him hit his opening tee shot and thought, 'Man, who is this kid?' We didn't know about him in America," McIlroy's third-round playing partner, Arron Oberholser, said. "If you had said his name to me a week before the tournament, I don't believe I would have known who he was. If he had won the British Amateur, for example, we would have known about him. So, quite honestly, he was this Northern Irish kid, and I didn't know who he was. I didn't even know how he got into the tournament."[xi]

McIlroy ended with a 72 to finish the 2007 Championship at +5, good enough for a tie for 42nd place. It was 12 shots behind the winner, Padraig Harrington, who beat Sergio Garcia in the playoff. Still, for McIlroy, it was an amazing introduction to the world stage. Everybody around the globe now knew who he was. He knew, going forward, that people would recognize him for the competitor he was.

"Hopefully, it's the shape of things to come," McIlroy said after winning the Silver Medal. "I think I'm getting better all the time, progressing as a player. Hopefully, I've got a few more Open Championships in me. It's a great performance, first major, first Open Championship, and hopefully I can go on to bigger and better things. I'm still the same old Rory McIlroy. I'll go up to Holywood Golf Club after this, I'll see my mates and stuff, and nothing will have changed. But I'm sure I'll probably have a bit more attention after the way I played this week. I'm sort of prepared for it, but it's still going to be a bit of a change for me."[xi]

Just two months later, on September 18, 2007, McIlroy reached a deal with International Sports Management and officially turned professional. He would make his debut at the British Masters. He also reached an agreement with agent Andrew "Chubby" Chandler, who had worked with Darren Clarke for years and had been negotiating with McIlroy on a contract. Chandler was very impressed with his new client.

"He was unbelievably confident," Chandler said when watching him at The Open. "He wasn't fazed at all by what was going on around him. He relished the attention. He had been born for that."[xi]

Chapter 4: Professional Career

Rookie Years (2007-08)

Rory McIlroy would begin his career on the European Tour, now known as the DP World Tour. He went through Tour school qualifying in early September and finished in a tie for 13th at The Oxfordshire, securing his card to play in Europe.

His goal, eventually, was to play on the PGA Tour, but he needed to work his way up to that. He would debut at the British Masters in 2009, playing at the infamous Belfry in England, host of many Ryder Cups.

McIlroy started his professional career with an opening round of 69 but followed it up with a disappointing 78. Fortunately, it was still good enough to play the weekend. After shooting 70 and 73 on the weekend, McIlroy finished in a tie for 42nd place, the same position he ended up at in the Open two months earlier.

From there, McIlroy only improved. He played the Alfred Dunhill Links Championship the following year and tied for third. He then finished in a tie for fourth at the Open de España. He would close out the season with a tie for 56th at the Portugal Masters.

McIlroy's 2008 season was a struggle, with him trying to push himself too hard. He had seen how Tiger exploded onto the scene after he turned professional and expected the same of himself. But it did not go so swimmingly, and Rory got frustrated with himself. In his first 11 tournaments in 2008, McIlroy failed to post a top-10 and missed five cuts. His best finish was a tie for 11th at the Abu Dhabi Championship, where he closed with 68 and 69. In April 2008, McIlroy admitted to having reached a boiling point where he lost his cool because he was so frustrated with his game.

"I'd just missed a few cuts in a row, and I was in Korea—Jeju Island—playing the Ballantyne Championship," McIlroy said. "And I missed the cut again. So, I was struggling. I had never felt so far from home and so lonely. I remember going back to my hotel room, at the end of the bed, crying, and I raided the mini-bar. Not the drinks. It was like Pringles, Coke, and Toblerone. I just remember this complete meltdown."xii

McIlroy got a good pep talk from his father, along with some of his mentors, including Clarke. By the end of the summer, things began to turn around, and McIlroy began to enjoy playing golf again.

He would feel at home when he played the Irish Open in May that year. McIlroy did not post any rounds over par, shooting 70-72-70-70 to post -6 and finish in a tie for seventh. It was his first top-10 that season—and his last one for quite a while.

McIlroy continued to battle himself. He missed two cuts in a row before tying for 10th at the European Open. He tried to qualify for the Open Championship at Royal Birkdale but failed, only frustrating him more. He then missed three more cuts in a row and was reeling. But then things began to turn around. Over the next five tournaments, McIlroy posted four top-10s, including a runner-up at the European Masters. Finally, he had some momentum, and he surged to the top 100 in the Official World Golf Ranking.

"This is how quick things can change in golf," he said. "So, (the meltdown) was in April 2008. Fast forward six months, to October '08, and I'm playing the Singapore Open. And I'm playing with Ernie Els in the third round. And we're in like the second-to-last group. I remember he hit driver off the first tee. And I'm like, 'Wow, this is so cool, I'm playing with Ernie Els.' He hit driver off the first tee, and I hit my three-wood past his driver. I was like, 'Oooh yeah, this is really cool.'"[xii]

2009-2010

McIlroy points to the start of 2009 as the time when things began clicking. It had taken him a year as a professional, but like many rookies, it takes a while to put it all together. McIlroy went to Hong Kong with a strong field and finished second alongside future major champion Francesco Molinari.

McIlroy had flown up the world rankings and was now in the top 50. He kept climbing with a third and fifth-place finish at the South African Open and Abu Dhabi Championship, respectively. The top-five finish at Abu Dhabi was especially impressive given the quality of the field, which included the likes of Louis Oosthuizen, Martin Kaymer, Sergio Garcia, Paul Casey, Padraig Harrington, and Colin Montgomerie.

The Dubai Desert Classic had a star-studded field when it kicked off at the end of January 2009. Many of the world's best were present, including Clarke, Lee Westwood, Garcia, Justin Rose, and Ernie Els. McIlroy surged to an opening-round lead with a round of 64. He followed it up with rounds of 68 and 67, finishing the third round in the fog to take a two-stroke lead into Sunday. He was on the precipice of his first professional victory.

McIlroy's final round was a roller coaster. He opened birdie-birdie-birdie before doubling the fifth. After bogeying the eighth to drop out of the lead, he surged back to the top with five straight birdies. But his big lead quickly dropped when he bogeyed holes 15 through 17. Still, he battled for a par on 18, getting up and down from a bunker, to finish one shot ahead of Rose for his first victory, making him the seventh-youngest champion at just 19 years old.

"This is my first win, and it's hard to win ... the first time always is," McIlroy said. "It's definitely a monkey off my back, having lost in playoffs twice. It's been an absolutely fantastic week."[xiii]

The victory was monumental for McIlroy. Given the quality of the field, the first-place finish meant a lot in terms of World Golf Ranking points. McIlroy surged all the way to 15th in the world, all but assuring him to play in all four major championships that year since the top-50 in the world get invitations.

"I think I have to reassess my goals now," McIlroy said. "But I go into every week with the same mindset. As long as I do that, I am happy. I knew sooner or later, I would be able to close one, and I am happy I did that this week."[xiii]

Prior to the Masters, McIlroy played in two World Golf Championship events, which included the best players in the world. In the World Match Play, McIlroy impressed by finishing in fifth place, making it all the way to the quarterfinals. He then finished 20th in the WGC-CA Championship.

McIlroy made his PGA Tour debut at The Honda Classic in March 2009 at Palm Beach Gardens in Florida. After a slow start, McIlroy put himself in contention by birdieing four of the final five holes on Friday. He would end up finishing in a tie for 13th, a solid start to his American career.

McIlroy tied for 19th at the Shell Houston Open in a tune-up for the Masters. He was now 18th in the world when he went to Augusta National for the first time. He was going along well for most of the first two days and had risen to sixth place on the leaderboard when he reached the 16th hole on Friday. But a double-bogey on 16 and then a bogey on 18 dropped him well back on the leaderboard. He would close with two sub-par rounds to tie for 20th, 10 shots behind champion Angel Cabrera.

McIlroy competed in his first Players Championship that May but missed the cut, followed by a disappointing finish at the Irish Open. But he then turned it around, going back to the European Tour and posting a 5th and 12th place finish at the BMW PGA Championship and European Open, respectively. He then played in his second major, the U.S. Open, and posted a T10 (tied for 10th) finish, his first top-10 in a major championship.

McIlroy's first real major success came at the PGA Championship in August at Hazeltine Country Club in Minnesota. Following a disappointing T47 at the Open Championship in Turnberry, Scotland, McIlroy posted four solid rounds at the PGA Championship. Although he never truly found himself in the mix, his final round 70 in very difficult conditions shot him up the leaderboard, finishing -3 and in a tie for third behind winner Y.E. Yang, who held on to beat Tiger Woods.

The PGA Championship seemed to springboard McIlroy, who posted seven top-seven finishes for the rest of the season in just eight events. He scored a fourth-place finish at the WGC-HSBC Champions tournament, which included the best players in the world. After a second-place finish at the Hong Kong Open, he tied for second at the Omega Mission Hills World Cup.

McIlroy had risen all the way to the top 10 of the World Golf Rankings by the start of 2010 and had earned his PGA Tour card. He would spend his next season playing between the PGA and European Tours.

Up until May, McIlroy failed to do much as he was struggling with a back injury that kept him from competing full-time. Despite posting a couple of top-10 finishes in the Middle East with impressive fields, he missed the cut at the Masters and the Houston Open in America. Then came the Quail Hollow Championship in Charlotte, North Carolina, in May.

2010 Quail Hollow Championship

McIlroy was still struggling with an ailing back and nearly withdrew from the event before it began.

"I had missed the cut at the Masters, and I was struggling with a bad back," McIlroy recalled. "I got an MRI scan when I went home, and it showed some stress around L4-L5, and the doctor told me it's probably better if you rest for a few weeks and not play."[xiv]

But McIlroy tested it out at Royal Portrush the week before and felt good enough to make the journey to the States to play. So, he decided to give it a go, not knowing what to expect.

He was getting a lot of treatment for it after his opening round 72, putting him well back of the lead. Through nine holes during the second round, he was at +3 and in serious danger of missing the cut. He would need a big rally on the back nine to play the weekend. He had to make up two shots to make the cut, and on the par-5 seventh, he hit what he coined as the "shot of the year," putting his long-iron shot to within a couple of feet from the hole and making eagle. He barely snuck in to make the weekend.[xv]

McIlroy's third round was topsy-turvy with a boatload of birdies mixed with a few bogeys. But a hot finish shot him up the leaderboard with a

66. He was now at -5 and four shots back from the lead with a group of players in front of him.

On Sunday, McIlroy opened with three pars before birdieing the fourth hole. Three more birdies going out got him to -9, and when he birdied the 11th hole, he found himself at -10 and tied for the lead with Angel Cabrera.

Then came one of the great closing stretches in PGA Tour history. McIlroy converted a birdie on the 14th and then struck a five-iron to within six feet on the par-5 15th hole. He made that for an eagle to put him eight strokes under par on the round and -13 for the tournament. But he was not done. He hit a beautiful iron out of a fairway bunker on 16 and converted yet another birdie to put him at -14 for the tournament, extending his lead.

On 18, McIlroy came 45 feet short of the hole with his approach and had a treacherous putt. Nonetheless, McIlroy rolled the putt perfectly, and when it found the center of the cup, the crowd let out a massive roar as McIlroy fired a fist pump into the air. It was a 10-under par 62, a score that would hold up; he had conquered his first PGA Tour victory.

"To win this tournament as my first is something quite special," Rory said after his win propelled him into the world's top 10. "I received so much support all day, and this crowd is quite special. It feels quite Augusta-like here. It's such a great tournament."[xv]

Many people point to the 2007 Open Championship as McIlroy's coming-out party, or his first win on the European Tour. But Rory signals this event as the one that really got his career going. It got massive media attention and really put him out there on the world stage as the next big thing in golf. And all this while playing in a tournament where he nearly withdrew because of a bad back!

"I remember getting to bed at like 2 a.m. I woke up the next day, playing with Anthony Kim, and I went out and played one of the rounds of my life and won my first PGA Tour event," McIlroy said. "It was an amazing day. It feels like such a long time ago, but at the same time, I can remember that. Those things stay with you, and I think part of the reason that I've played so well here since is I had such positive momentum, those positive memories, and every time I come here, those good feelings get rekindled. It's been a good place for me."[xv]

2010 Open Championship and PGA Championship

After his win at Quail Hollow, McIlroy posted a top-10 at the Memorial Tournament before struggling at Pebble Beach in the U.S. Open and missing the cut. But prior to playing in the Open Championship at St. Andrew's, he was encouraged after finishing in fourth place in France.

The conditions were perfect for the first round of the Open Championship as McIlroy drew an early tee time. Now 21 years old, he went out and flat-out decimated St. Andrew's, using his power to take apart the short-4s around the infamous loop of the Old Course. After a birdie on 16, McIlroy was -8 for the round; no one in major championship history had ever shot a 10-under round or a 62. He was on the precipice of shooting both. The 18th was a short par-4 and was basically a gimme birdie. But the Road Hole 17th was notoriously difficult to conquer.

McIlroy struck an iron to within a few feet on 17, and the 62 was in play. However, shockingly, McIlroy missed the short putt. He went on to birdie the 18th for a 63, tying the record for lowest score in a major championship. He would lead by two shots over Louis Oosthuizen after the first round.

The weather during the second round on Friday was brutal, though. Oosthuizen went out early before conditions got tough and surged to -10, ahead of McIlroy, who was teeing off just as the wind picked up in full force. The wind got so strong that play at one point during the round had to be stopped because balls were rolling off the green. When it resumed, it got the best of McIlroy, who plummeted down the leaderboard with an 81. He just barely survived the cut.

"It was not a great one," McIlroy said. "It was so tough out there. It was so hard to get anywhere near the pins with the crosswinds. You didn't know if you could even ground your putter. It was just a very testing day."[xvi]

If not for that horrible round and the meddlesome interference of Mother Nature, McIlroy would have won the Open that year at St.

Andrew's. He bounced back with rounds of 69-68 (-7) to finish the tournament at -8, tying him for third. While it was eight shots behind Oosthuizen, who won by an incredible seven shots, it was an amazing bounce back after a second-round 81. McIlroy ended up shooting -17 for three of his four rounds.

McIlroy again found himself fighting for his first major championship less than a month later at Whistling Straits in Wisconsin at the PGA Championship. After a 71 in the opening round, McIlroy followed it up with rounds of 68 and 67 to put him at -10 and in a tie for second going into the final day. He was three shots behind leader Nick Watney.

Watney imploded on Sunday, and McIlroy found himself tied for the lead on the back nine of a crowded leaderboard that included the likes of Dustin Johnson, Bubba Watson, Jason Day, and Martin Kaymer. But a disappointing bogey on 15 dropped McIlroy to -10, one behind Kaymer, who would go on to post -11. McIlroy was unable to birdie the closing holes and would finish one shot back of Kaymer, who went on to win the championship in a playoff over Watson. It was McIlroy's second consecutive top-3 finish in a major.

McIlroy's success earned him his first Ryder Cup invitation in 2010. He would go 1-1-2, having Stewart Cink in Sunday's singles. The Europeans would go on to win the Ryder Cup in a dramatic finish in which fellow countryman Graeme McDowell defeated Hunter Mahan in the competition's final match.

McIlroy finished the 2010 season with a string of top-10 finishes, setting him up for a big 2011 season.

2011 Masters

McIlroy had a quiet start to the 2011 season, playing very sparingly as he continued to recover from the back injury that had bothered him in 2010. Going into the 2011 Masters, McIlroy had a T17, T70, and T10 in three PGA Tour events. Thus, expectations were not high going into the Masters.

But McIlroy opened the Masters with a spectacular 7-under 65 to put him atop the leaderboard. For three days, he never fell from that top position. He shot a 69 on Friday to put him at -10 and then a 70 on Saturday to position himself at -12, four shots ahead of Angel Cabrera, K.J. Choi, Charl Schwartzel, and Jason Day going into Sunday.

"It's a great position to be in. I'm finally feeling comfortable on this golf course," McIlroy told reporters after his third round.[xvii]

Many labeled this performance reminiscent of Tiger Woods' glorious 1997 Masters, wherein he won by 12 shots, finishing at -18. While McIlroy's margin of victory was not expected to be as big, he was dominating Augusta National, and many were putting the green jacket on him before he even teed off on Sunday.

But as McIlroy was teeing off that Sunday, roars were generating all around Augusta National. First, Tiger Woods, who started at -5, was making a run up the leaderboard. Then, Schwartzel chipped in off the green at the first and then holed out for eagle on three to get to -11. So, when McIlroy three-putted the opening hole, he had already lost his four-shot lead and was tied with Schwartzel.

Frustrations mounted as McIlroy failed to bogey the easy par-5 second. He failed to get anything going on the front and sat at -11 after nine holes, just one ahead of Woods, Cabrera, and Schwartzel.

Then, everything came apart at 10. McIlroy hit one of the worst duck hooks you will ever see, and his ball landed near a group of houses some 300 yards from the hole. He continued to hit the ball all over the place at 10, and after missing a short putt for a double-bogey, he walked off with a triple to drop to -8. Things just kept unraveling from there. He missed a short par putt on 11 and then four-putted the 12th.

The pressure had gotten to him. Rory looked dazed and confused, and on his face, you could see he had lost all confidence in his game. He was clearly rattled.

On the 13th hole, McIlroy hit another pull off the tee that landed in the creek. Knowing his tournament was over, McIlroy sank his face into his arm for the world to see. It was an unfortunate meltdown from one of the world's best young stars. McIlroy would walk off the 18th hole with an 80, 10 shots behind the champion Schwartzel. After the round, McIlroy was in tears as he called his parents, dismayed by what had occurred. But after some encouragement, he faced the media and had an optimistic view of his future.

"I was leading this golf tournament with nine holes to go, and I just unraveled. It's a Sunday at a major, what it can do," he said. "This is my first experience at it, and hopefully, the next time I'm in this position, I'll be able to handle it a little better. I didn't handle it particularly well today, obviously, but it was a character-building day. I'll come out stronger for it."[xvii]

2011 U.S. Open

A fifth-place finish at the Memorial Tournament and a couple of top-10s in Europe gave McIlroy some confidence heading into the U.S. Open at Congressional Country Club in Bethesda, Maryland. He had to endure questions that entire week about his Masters meltdown, and he knew the only way to put that behind him was to put up a stellar performance at the U.S. Open. He would do just that.

The track was extremely soft, which benefited McIlroy's ball-striking ability. He stuck several irons close to the hole. He surged to the top of the leaderboard with a first-round 65, three ahead of the field. He then went out on Saturday and continued his hot play. On the par-4 sixth hole, McIlroy hit the shot of the tournament. With his second shot, he flew his ball to the back of the green on purpose, letting it ride the slope down the hill. The ball slowly moved backward until it finally reached the bottom of the cup for an eagle. McIlroy would finish with a 66 to open up a six-shot lead on Y.E. Yang.

Rory kept his foot on the gas on Saturday, continuing to grow his lead. In what many called a Tiger-like performance, he was -14 at the close of play and had an eight-shot lead over Yang. He was in complete cruise control.

Unlike the Masters, McIlroy never crashed and burned on Sunday. In fact, he shot his fourth straight round in the 60s, a rarity at the U.S. Open. He tapped in for par on the 18th hole for a final round 69 to finish at -16, eight shots ahead of Jason Day. With that, Rory McIlroy had won his first major championship in dominant fashion.

"I felt like I got over the Masters pretty quickly. I kept telling you guys that, and I don't know if you believed me or not. But here you go," McIlroy said, gesturing to the shiny prize on the table. "Nice to prove some people wrong."[xviii]

As an added bonus, the U.S. Open win happened to occur on Father's Day, and the victory was extra special for Rory and his father Gerry, who fondly remembered his phone call with Rory after that Masters debacle.

"I said, 'Rory, are you OK, son?' Because you always fear for your kids," Gerry said. "And he says, 'Dad, um, I have no problem with it at all. I hit a few bad shots. And if you play golf, then you'll understand that.'"[xviii]

The victory sent shockwaves across the PGA Tour that the next big superstar had arrived. This was far more than just a win, as McIlroy had completely obliterated U.S. Open scoring records. His 16-under-par was the lowest 72-hole score in tournament history, far surpassing the field at a championship well-known for its extreme physical as well as mental challenges.

McIlroy's fellow countryman and close friend, Graeme McDowell, who had won the U.S. Open in 2010, had nothing but praise for his friend.

"Nothing this kid does ever surprises me," McDowell said. "He's the best player I've ever seen. I didn't have a chance to play with Tiger when he was in his real pomp, and this guy is the best I've ever seen. Simple as that. He's great for golf. He's a breath of fresh air for the game, and perhaps we're ready for golf's next superstar. And maybe, Rory is it."[xviii]

2012 Honda Classic: Rory vs. Tiger

Following McIlroy's victory at Congressional, he was an overwhelming favorite to win the Open Championship at Royal St. George's. However, he never contended. He played with young American superstar Rickie Fowler in a third round that was met with torrential rain and wind. He would finish well back of eventual winner Darren Clarke. He also never contended at the PGA Championship.

The 2012 season got off to an amazing start for McIlroy. He posted five consecutive top-five finishes to open the year, including a runner-up finish at the WGC-World Match Play Championships. He went into the Honda Classic at Palm Beach Gardens, Florida, with a chance to take over the world's No. 1 ranking.

41

McIlroy led most of the way and seemed to be cruising to an easy victory when Tiger Woods made an epic charge. Tiger, who was several holes ahead of McIlroy, hit a spectacular wood onto the par-5 18th and then sank the eagle putt, sending out an enormous roar that reverberated back to McIlroy. McIlroy's lead on the tough course dwindled to one stroke.

"I could hear the huge roar," McIlroy said. "And it definitely wasn't a birdie roar."[xix]

But McIlroy did not fold. He rolled in a birdie putt on 13 to go up by two, and then made three incredible saves on 14, 15, and 17 to hold that lead. After parring 18, he had survived Tiger Woods' charge and finally took his place as the world's No. 1 golfer.

"It was tough today, especially seeing Tiger make a charge," McIlroy said. "I knew par golf would probably be good enough. To shoot 1 under in these conditions, when you go into the round with the lead, is very nice. And I was just able to get the job done."[xix]

With that accomplishment, Rory McIlroy became the 16th player to be ranked the world's No. 1 golfer, and the second-youngest behind only Tiger, who became No. 1 when he was 21.

2012 PGA Championship

After gaining the world's No. 1 ranking, McIlroy hit a slump. He tied for 40th in his return to Augusta National, and then missed cuts at the Players Championship, Memorial, and U.S. Open. He did not compete at the Open Championship, either. His last chance to claim a major championship would come at Kiawah Island, South Carolina, in August.

McIlroy opened with an impressive 67 to put him one shot behind Sweden's Carl Pettersson after the opening round. But the wind blew hard in Round 2, and McIlroy's 75 sent him back to -2. But he was still only two shots back of the lead, since the whole field came crashing down in the high winds as Mother Nature once again asserted her dominion.

McIlroy surged to the top of the leaderboard in the third round, going ahead just after a weather delay halfway through his day. He finished strong Sunday morning to shoot a 67 and stand three clear of Pettersson going into the final round.

McIlroy birdied the first two holes in the final round to extend his lead, and then he added another birdie on the par-5 seventh to move to -10 and six clear of the field. He stayed in attack mode, and after a birdie on the par-5 16th hole, Rory was sitting at -12 and seven shots ahead.

After just missing the green on his approach to the 18th hole, McIlroy took his putter out and rolled the ball from the fringe and sank the putt. He gave a big fist pump as soon as the putt went in. McIlroy shot a final round 66 and finished -13, winning the PGA Championship by a record eight shots, the same margin he had won the U.S. Open by a year ago.

"To sit up here," McIlroy said, "and see this trophy and call myself a multiple Major Champion, I know I've talked about it in the past, and not many people have done it, and yeah, I'm very privileged to join such an elite list of names."[xx]

McIlroy had come a long way from his collapse at the 2011 Masters. In the two majors that he seized the lead in on the weekend, he only extended his lead and decimated the field.

"I learned a lot from the Masters last year," McIlroy said. "There's quite a bit of relief to get the second one out of the way. But you know, just so happy that I was able to play like this and win another major."[xx]

The Ryder Cup would be the perfect finish to a spectacular year for McIlroy. The Europeans were getting crushed by the Americans at Medinah Country Club in Illinois. McIlroy and Ian Poulter teamed up to get a late point on Saturday to give the team hope going into Sunday. Trailing 10-6, McIlroy went out third and faced Keegan Bradley in singles. Interestingly enough, he almost missed his tee time, as the hotel he was staying at was in the Eastern time zone, but the course itself was in the Central time zone. Luckily, he made it just in time—with a much-appreciated police escort!

The help from Illinois' finest was not in vain. On the 17th hole, McIlroy won 2 and 1. In fact, the first five matches all went to Europe, shifting the momentum of that Ryder Cup completely. When Martin Kaymer sank his putt on 18 to beat Steve Stricker, the Europeans had pulled off one of the biggest upsets in Ryder Cup history. It would be dubbed "The Miracle at Medinah."

A Rough 2013 & Magical 2014

Rory McIlroy went on a roll following his 2012 PGA Championship victory and again sat on top of the world after winning back-to-back FedEx Cup Playoff events, the Deutsche Bank Championship, and the BMW Championship. He also won the DP Tour World Championship in Dubai in November 2012. He was dominating golf and establishing himself as a true icon of the game.

But McIlroy suddenly lost his steam in 2013, failing to win on the PGA Tour and posting just four top-10s. He had a horrible outing at Muirfield at the Open Championship, where he missed the cut, finishing +12 in difficult conditions. He also failed to post any victories on the DP World Tour, making him completely winless on the season. He had also lost his world No. 1 ranking.

So, what was going on with Rory in 2013 that led to such a subpar year? As it turned out, a number of things may have contributed to his struggles.

First and perhaps foremost, he had just inked a lucrative sponsorship deal with Nike—but with some grave, unforeseen repercussions. The deal saw him abandon his long-time Titleist equipment, but it seemed that getting used to his new Nike clubs turned out to be much more difficult than he had anticipated. He struggled to adapt to the new equipment, which led to rampant frustration. His swing was off, his confidence wavered, and his game was plagued with inconsistencies throughout the year.

Then, added to that was the fact that he was embroiled in a lawsuit with his former management company, Horizon Sports, over excessive fees, misleading contracts, and a lack of proper representation. It was an ugly drama that would finally come to end in an out-of-court settlement in 2015.

Additionally, Rory was in a very high-profile relationship with tennis star Caroline Wozniacki, a romance that began in 2011 but would fall apart in 2014.

And finally, added to all of that, some questionable early-season scheduling decisions seemed to have had a negative impact as well, as some pundits observed that it had left him unprepared and out of shape. All in all, it was a year that the young phenom would probably prefer to forget!

After such a daunting and disheartening year, some professional golfers might find themselves on a continued slide into decline and irrelevance, but not Rory McIlroy. Looking toward 2014, Rory had nothing but optimism—and it was not misplaced.

McIlroy would see a remarkable turnaround in 2014. He won the BMW Championship in Europe, one of the DP World Tour's premium events. He posted four straight top-10 finishes on the PGA Tour, including a

T8 at the Masters and T23 at the U.S. Open. He went to the Open Championship at Royal Liverpool with high expectations, knowing he was playing stellar golf.

McIlroy blitzed to the top of the leaderboard in Round 1, making six birdies and no bogeys. His 66 was one better than Italy's Matteo Manassero and three better than Tiger Woods, who was just returning from back surgery.

With much of the attention on Tiger in Round 2, who ended up faltering, McIlroy quietly went out and took apart Royal Liverpool for the second straight day. He shot another 66 to get to -12 and open up a four-shot lead over Dustin Johnson and five shots over the likes of Sergio Garcia, Louis Oosthuizen, and Francesco Molinari. McIlroy was in cruise control through those two days, reminiscent of his previous two major victories.

But McIlroy started off slowly in Round 3. He was actually caught from behind by Rickie Fowler, who was seven-under on his round through 12 holes and reached -12. On the par 3 11th hole, McIlroy faced an almost impossible chip shot and was on the verge of losing his lead. But he got it to within 12 feet and then sank his putt for par.

"It was a big putt to save par. I felt quite nervous," McIlroy said. "I tried to take the end result out of my mind. I focused on a spot two or three inches in front of the ball. I said, 'Right, all you need to do is roll it over your spot.' That's all I kept telling myself. 'Roll it over your spot. Roll it over your spot.'"[xxi]

Many experts point to that one moment as the turning point of the entire championship. Fowler cooled down over the stretch, dropping to -10. McIlroy, leading Fowler by two, then buried an eagle putt on 16. After hitting two beautiful shots onto the par-18th green, he sank the eagle putt to close out a 68 and carry a six-shot lead into Sunday.

McIlroy started off slowly again and watched a surging Sergio Garcia pull within two shots of the lead on Sunday. Nonetheless, slowly but surely, Rory was able to close the door and not make any mistakes. He held off Fowler and Garcia to finish -17 and win by two. It was McIlroy's third major championship, and he was now a Masters title away from the career grand slam. McIlroy credited his putting performance, traditionally a weakness, for his Open triumph.

"I was just picking a spot on the green and trying to roll it over my spot, roll it over my spot every time. I wasn't thinking about holing it. I wasn't thinking about what it would mean, or how many further clear it would get me. I just wanted to roll that ball over that spot. If that went in, then great. If it didn't, then I'd try it the next hole."[xxi]

Less than one month later, McIlroy went to Valhalla Country Club as confident as could be. He had not only won the Open Championship, but he also defeated the top players in golf at the WGC-Bridgestone Invitational. He was seeking his third straight win at the PGA Championship and was the tournament favorite.

Just like at the Open and his other major triumphs, McIlroy got off to a blistering start. He shot a 66 to sit in second place after the first round.

He followed that up with a 67 to take the lead at -9, one shot over Jason Day and Jim Furyk. After a 67 in the third round, he was -13 and one clear of Bernd Wiesberger and two ahead of Rickie Fowler.

But McIlroy started slowly in Round 4 and was passed by both Fowler and Phil Mickelson, who got off to lightning-fast starts. As Rory sat in the fairway at the par-5 10th, he was trailing Fowler by three shots. He took out a three-wood and hit the shot of the tournament, a low runner that just kept rolling until it stopped about seven feet away from the cup. He converted the eagle and, just like that, he was within one of the lead.

"The eagle on 10 was massive," explained McIlroy. "I started the round very tentatively. I just didn't really have it. Sort of just trying to get through the first few holes making pars while everyone else was attacking, so that wasn't good. But the eagle on 10 just changed everything. I hit a three-wood from I think it was 284 (yards) total. The ball flight was probably around 30 feet lower than I intended. And the line of the shot was probably around 15 yards left of where I intended. It was lucky, it really was. You need a little bit of luck in major championships to win and that was my lucky break."[xxii]

A weather delay on Sunday afternoon then pushed the tournament to the brink of having to finish on Monday with little daylight left. But the players were pushing to finish. McIlroy hit his approach to the 13th close and converted the birdie while Fowler bogeyed the hole ahead. McIlroy was now one ahead of Fowler and Mickelson.

With it now getting darker by the minute, McIlroy extended his lead with a gorgeous birdie on 17. Players were rushing to get in as it got very dark. McIlroy nearly was hit with disaster when his drive on 18 flirted with the water but barely stayed dry. Up ahead, Mickelson just missed converting his eagle chip but tapped in for a birdie to put pressure on McIlroy. Despite the encroaching twilight, McIlroy was able to get on the green in three and then cozied his birdie putt to within a couple of feet. Under a fierce, gloaming sky, McIlroy tapped in for the par and celebrated his fourth major championship. It was his second that season.

"He's better than everyone else right now," Mickelson said.[xxii]

"He's on a roll. He is the best player in the world and just playing phenomenal golf," said Henrik Stenson, who was also in contention. "It's always hard to compare players. If he's not the same [as Woods], he's not far behind. He's got every opportunity to move on from here on."[xxii]

McIlroy became the seventh player in history to win the final two major championships of the year, and the first since Padraig Harrington did it in 2008. After a dreary 2013, he was back at the top of his game in 2014.

"I guess it just makes me realize that even though last year wasn't the year I wanted, the last three or four years have been very, very good," McIlroy said. "It gives me even more motivation to go on and work harder and try to win more tournaments, more majors, and be involved in more Ryder Cups like last week."[xxiii]

McIlroy finished as runner-up in his final two European events and made three top-10s on the PGA Tour. However, he finished second in the Tour Championship, coming up just short of winning the FedEx Cup.

The magical year concluded with Rory McIlroy being named the PGA Tour Player of the Year and also being presented with the Jack Nicklaus Award. He was the No. 1 player in the world and perched at the top of golf at this moment.

Many experts say that 2014 was his best professional year to date.

Highlights from 2015-2018

By 2015, McIlroy had established himself again as the best player in the world and sat atop the world golf rankings. In January 2015, in a star-studded field at the Dubai Desert Classic, McIlroy opened with rounds of 66 64-66 to open up a big lead. Despite a final round of 70, McIlroy cruised to a victory to only further cement himself as the world's best player.

In April, McIlroy embarked upon the Augusta National in his first attempt to win the career grand slam. But the story instead would shift to another young star in the making—Jordan Spieth. The young 21-year-old American dominated the competition, tying Tiger Woods'

Masters scoring record of -18. McIlroy never contended, but he did shoot a final round 66 to finish in fourth place.

With the storylines all focused on Spieth, Rory sought to show that he was still the best in the world. He proved that at the Cadillac Match Play, which included the top 64 players in the world. Played at Harding Park in San Francisco, McIlroy went 3-0 in round-robin play to advance to the Round of 16. He then crushed Hideki Matsuyama 6 and 5 before winning a 22-hole marathon against Paul Casey in the quarterfinals that extended into the next morning. He then beat Jim Furyk in the semifinals and cruised to victory over Gary Woodland in the championship match to win his first World Match Play title. The win extended McIlroy's point margin as world No. 1. He also became the first player not named Tiger Woods to win the event as the No. 1 seed.

"I'm really proud of myself with how I showed a lot of character early in the tournament, coming back from some deficits," McIlroy said. "I played really solid golf. I have got on a nice little run in match play. I got a lot of confidence from the way I played against Rickie [Fowler] in the Ryder Cup last year [winning 5 and 4] and just followed it on through into this."[xxiv]

The 2015 U.S. Open was played under difficult course conditions at Chambers Bay in University Place, Washington. Played in high elevation, the course was dried out and very rough after a period of unusually high heat and drought. This caused the green's native fescue grass to turn brown and wither, while only a very bumpy poa annua grass thrived, leading to inconsistent and unpredictable putting surfaces. This garnered a great deal of controversy and would ultimately cause Chambers Bay to be removed from the USGA's list of potential future venues.

McIlroy was +4 going into the final round, eight back of the leaders and seemingly out of it. But he then birdied 6 of his first 13 holes to vault into contention at -2, just three back of Dustin Johnson at the time. However, he struggled down the stretch, bogeying twice to finish even par and in a tie for ninth. For the second straight major, Jordan Spieth came out on top after Johnson collapsed on the back nine.

McIlroy was eager to defend his Open Championship title but instead had to withdraw after suffering a severe ankle sprain while playing soccer with friends a couple of weeks prior to the major. It was very disappointing, especially given McIlroy's recent success at St. Andrew's. Instead, he could only watch on television as Spieth just missed out on winning a third major in a row; Zach Johnson would win his second major in a playoff.

When McIlroy did return about seven weeks later, he showed some rust. He finished 17th at the PGA Championship and never made much of a run at the FedEx Cup. However, he did go on to win the DP Tour's biggest prize, finishing in first place at the DP Tour World Championship, and as a result, winning the coveted Race to Dubai. In what was a crazy year-and-a-half, he was ready to take a bit of a break following the win that had earned him $3 million.

"I really feel, even though I've had a few weeks off over the summer, I need this period just to reflect on things and re-evaluate how I want to go forward," McIlroy said. "I'm happy that this was my last event of the year and I've done really well. I've ended the season on a high and I'm happy to put the clubs away for a while."[xxv]

McIlroy struggled in the majors in 2016. While posting a top-10 at the Masters wherein he never really contended, he missed the cut at the U.S. Open and PGA Championship. His best finish was a tie for fifth at the Open Championship, but he was 16 shots back of the winner, Henrik Stenson.

McIlroy had two big moments in 2016. The first was a victory at the Irish Open, played close to home. It had always been his dream to win this event, and he finished -12, three shots clear of the field.

The second big moment occurred at East Lake Golf Club just outside of Atlanta, Georgia. McIlroy entered the Tour Championship in sixth position after having just won the Deutsche Bank Championship, and he had to get some help to win the FedEx Cup. McIlroy made an epic back-nine charge as he tried to catch Kevin Chappell. On the 16th, McIlroy holed out from the fairway for an eagle two to get within one. He birdied 18 to shoot 64, and thus forced a three-way playoff with Chappell and Ryan Moore.

McIlroy and Moore would end up going four playoff holes after Chappell was eliminated after the first. On the fourth playoff hole,

McIlroy drained a 15-foot birdie putt to not only win the tournament but also claim the FedEx Cup title and $10 million.

"I couldn't have imagined six weeks ago, after Baltusrol (PGA Championship), I would be FedEx Cup champion," McIlroy said. "I feel my game is really coming together at the right time, and two wins in the last three feels pretty nice."[xxvi]

At the Ryder Cup, McIlroy and the Europeans lost the Ryder Cup for the first time since 2008, getting crushed by the American squad. It was the first time Rory had lost as a member of the European Ryder Cup team.

McIlroy's 2017 season was largely one to forget. In January, he was diagnosed with a stress fracture in his rib that would cause him persistent pain and hamper him throughout the year. He also changed clubs again that year, moving on to a TaylorMade sponsorship when Nike stopped producing golf equipment. Added to that, he changed caddies after nine years when that relationship had become strained.

So, for the first time since 2013, McIlroy failed to post a victory on either the PGA or European Tour. He never contended at the Masters despite finishing in a tie for seventh. He would miss the cut at the 2017 U.S. Open, although he made a decent Sunday charge at the Open Championship, finishing in a tie for fourth behind winner Jordan Spieth. He would then finish in a tie for 22nd at the PGA Championship at Quail Hollow. The most disappointing stretch came at the end of the year when he failed to qualify for the Tour Championship, finishing outside of the top 30.

The No. 1 ranking was long gone, and Rory had to try to regroup. Of course, going through ups and downs is nothing new for golfers. They go through swing changes, suffer myriad injuries, and often find themselves up one year and down the next. Since 2014, McIlroy had gone through a notably long stretch of consistency at the top, but he was now in a slump. However, it would not last long.

McIlroy started 2018 with a third- and second-place finish at the Abu Dhabi Championship and Dubai Desert Classic, two tournaments with prestigious fields. After struggling in his first four starts on the PGA Tour, he went to the Arnold Palmer Invitational seeking a win. The tournament was extra special because Palmer had just passed away. Names like Tiger Woods and Phil Mickelson had entered the event, making it a strong field.

McIlroy barely survived the cut but shot a third-round 67 to put himself into contention. Going into the final round, McIlroy found himself two shots behind Henrik Stenson and one behind Bryson DeChambeau and Ryan Moore. And then, just like at Quail Hollow where he got his first PGA Tour victory, he put together one of those iconic final round charges he was so well-known for.

It started at the sixth hole, where McIlroy went on a run, birdieing four holes in a row. He then chipped in for a birdie at 13 and drained another from 20 feet out on 14. After a birdie on 16 and a par on 17, McIlroy sat at -17 for the tournament and in the lead. From 25 feet out, McIlroy made his eighth birdie of the day and claimed his first victory since 2016. The final round 64 was good enough to win by three strokes.

"To be able to create my own little piece of history on the 18th green here was pretty special," McIlroy said. "I'm just so happy to be back in the winner's circle again and win a tournament that has Arnold Palmer's name on it, someone that means so much to us in the game of golf."[xxvii]

Talk of a career grand slam heated up at the Masters when McIlroy found himself in the hunt. Playing with Spieth in the third round, Rory went out and shot a 65 to put himself in second place, three shots behind leader Patrick Reed, whom he would play with on Sunday.

But after birdieing the first two holes to get within one of the lead, McIlroy's charge stalled. He dropped three shots from the 5th to the 12th hole while Reed surged ahead. McIlroy would finish in a tie for fifth, six shots behind Reed.

McIlroy had a horrific U.S. Open at Shinnecock Hills, finishing +10 and missing the cut. Nonetheless, he found himself in the mix alongside Tiger Woods and Jordan Spieth at the Open Championship at Carnoustie. However, Francesco Molinari had a phenomenal Sunday playing with Woods and went on to capture the Claret Jug. A tie for seventh at the Tour Championship ended McIlroy's season, where he posted just one victory along with eight top-10s.

Turnaround Season–2019

McIlroy had made progress in 2018 in his quest to return to the top, and he continued that momentum to post four victories in 2019. He was very consistent early in the year, posting five consecutive top-six finishes going into the Players Championship in May. A win at Ponte Vedra would put him back at No. 1 in the world.

McIlroy had never played well at the Players, but he was in excellent form and found himself in the game early after a first-round 67. After firing a second-round 65, he was tied for the lead after two rounds with Tommy Fleetwood.

Cool, cloudy conditions in Florida that weekend made the Sunshine State feel more like Northern Ireland for Rory. He shot 70 on Saturday but was passed by Jon Rahm, who put up an amazing 64 to sit at -15, one ahead of Fleetwood and McIlroy.

McIlroy looked to be out of it when he put his second shot in the water on 12, dropping him to -12. But Rahm was also struggling, and through nine holes, McIlroy was still just one back. McIlroy then made a charge, birdieing 11, 12, and 16 to get to -16 and pass Jim Furyk, who had posted -15. Meanwhile, Rahm was falling apart after putting his second into the water on 11. McIlroy parred 17 and 18 to post -16 and win the Players Championship for the first time. This win was extra special for him, given that it landed on St. Patrick's Day.

"This is probably the deepest field of the year, with so much on the line," McIlroy, now 29 years old, said. "I'm thankful it was my turn this week."[xxviii]

McIlroy continued to showcase incredible consistency in 2019. He posted a top-10 at the World Match Play before tying for 21st at the Masters, a championship won by Tiger Woods. Then, he recorded two consecutive top-10s at the PGA Championship and Wells Fargo Championship before winning the RBC Canadian Open for his second victory of the year.

But McIlroy's biggest disappointment came at the Open Championship. For the first time, he got to play the major championship in his home country, as it was held at Royal Portrush in Northern Ireland. Fans lined up early just to catch a glimpse of their hometown hero and cheer him on. It was the same course he shot a 61 at as a teenager, breaking the course record.

However, the pressure of high expectations got the best of Rory. He put his opening tee shot out of bounds, and everything just derailed from there. He got a quadruple-bogey 8 on the first hole en route to an ugly eight-over 79. Then, despite a better second round, he missed the cut—a real shocker to the golfing world, to be sure! McIlroy's close friend and fellow Irishman Shane Lowry would win the Claret Jug.

Nonetheless, McIlroy quickly shook off that disappointment. He finished the year strong by winning the Tour Championship by three shots over Xander Schauffele and capturing his second FedEx Cup title.

Despite not winning any majors, McIlroy had a Players title and FedEx Cup, and thus, was named the PGA Tour Player of the Year. This came as somewhat of a surprise, as many thought Brooks Koepka would win the award after having won the PGA Championship. But Rory McIlroy's consistency all year reigned supreme.

"I'm very humbled and very honored," McIlroy said. "It validates some of the decisions I made to start the year, and I couldn't be more proud."[xxix]

Close Calls at Majors 2020-2024

McIlroy went into the 2020 season on a five-year major championship drought. Despite having won the 2019 Players Championship, FedEx Cup, and the Player of the Year Award, the media began putting more pressure on him regarding the tournament's big events. Once seemingly a lock to get to get to 10 majors, McIlroy was stuck on just 4.

The 2020 season presented an even bigger challenge: COVID-19. The pandemic forced the cancellation of the Players Championship and the Open Championship and paused the season for nearly three months. On top of that, Rory's typical inclination to travel between the PGA Tour and DP World Tour was halted due to travel restrictions.

Prior to COVID-19, McIlroy was on absolute fire, entering seven events and finishing in the top-five in every single one. In a top-field event, he won the World Golf Championships-HSBC Champions, only increasing his lead as the world's best player. But the pandemic break affected Rory considerably. He had been on top of his game, yet when he returned from a three-month layoff, he looked rusty and out of sync.

All the major championships were pushed back until the late summer and fall. He finished T33 at the PGA Championship in August, T8 at the U.S. Open in September, and T5 at the Masters in November. The major drought continued into 2021. McIlroy also failed to defend his FedEx Cup, finishing T8 at the Tour Championship.

Things more or less went back to normal by the time 2021 rolled around, however. McIlroy got off to a slow start in the year, missing the cut at the Players and Masters Tournament. Then, after winning the Wells Fargo Championship for the second time, he finished a distant 49th at the PGA Championship. But he nonetheless found himself in the hunt at the U.S. Open in June at Torrey Pines, California.

After seemingly out of it with rounds of 70-73 to put him six back of the lead after two rounds, McIlroy went out on "Moving Day" and posted a 67 to get him to -3. It helped that the leaders struggled on the tough course, and by the end of the round, McIlroy sat just two back of the lead held by Louis Oosthuizen, Russell Henley, and Mackenzie Hughes.

McIlroy went out and shot one-under on the front nine in the final round to put him at -4 and in second place behind Oosthuizen. It was a star-studded leaderboard as the back nine got underway with names like DeChambeau, Rahm, Koepka, Morikawa, McIlroy, and Oosthuizen all right there near the top. Unfortunately, McIlroy's hopes collapsed after a bogey on 11 and then a double-bogey on the treacherous 12th. He dropped to -1 and finished alone in sixth, five shots behind the eventual winner, Rahm.

McIlroy's struggles at the Open Championship continued with a T46 at Royal St. George's. He then represented Ireland in the Olympics that summer in Tokyo, Japan, and failed to medal, finishing in fourth place.

McIlroy's quest for his first major in eight years continued in 2022. In all four majors, he would be right there at the end, particularly in two of them. He went into the Masters still searching for the career grand slam and posted his best finish yet. Although he never really contended, he vaulted into second place, well behind winner Scottie Scheffler, who dominated the competition that week. McIlroy next went to Southern Hills and posted an eighth-place finish at the PGA Championship.

McIlroy went into the U.S. Open at Brookline Country Club in Massachusetts in terrific form, just coming off his second victory at the RBC Canadian Open. He posted a first-round 67 to put himself just one back of the lead after the opening round.

McIlroy was still one back after two rounds, but difficult conditions in Round 3 saw him drop down the leaderboard. He would finish with a round 73 to slip to a tie for seventh, three back of the leader Matt Fitzpatrick.

McIlroy's putter went stale on Sunday. He got to -2 and was within striking distance of the lead, but could not get any closer to the group up top. Despite a final round 69, McIlroy finished at -2, three back of the winner Fitzpatrick and in a tie for fifth.

It looked like McIlroy's major drought would end at the Open Championship, though, at St. Andrew's. The last time he played at St. Andrew's, it was one round that swept him away. He was -17 for three of the rounds, but an 81 in heavy winds ruined his hopes. He would continue his success at St. Andrew's in 2022. He shot an opening round 66 and followed it with a 68 to put him at -10, just three back of the leader, Cameron Smith.

McIlroy put on a show in the third round. He was three-under for the round at the turn and sat at -13, one back of Viktor Hovland. However, he was buried right square in a fairway bunker at the short par-4 10th. That was when he provided some magic.

Rory splashed the shot out, got it over the lip, watched it land five feet short of the hole, and then saw it trickle its way into the cut for an eagle two. The crowd roared as McIlroy sent up a fist pump. That breathtaking shot vaulted him into the lead. He would go on to shoot 66 and sit at -16, tied with Hovland after three rounds. The next closest players were Smith and Cameron Young at -12.

But to win at St. Andrew's in easy conditions, you had to keep making birdies. Sadly, that did not happen for McIlroy on Sunday. He missed birdie putt after birdie putt. His putter deserted him at the worst time.

He never made a bogey all day, but made just two birdies. Usually, that would be great; however, Cameron Smith was making everything and surged past him into the lead.

"I tried to stay as patient as possible, and I kept hitting good putts," McIlroy said. "I hit a good putt on 13, 14, 15, 16, 17. I was hitting good putts. They just were not dropping. It's hard, like, there's a lot of putts today where I couldn't just trust myself to start it inside the hole. I was always starting it on the edge or just outside thinking it was going to move. More times than not, they just sort of stayed there."xxx

It was just not meant to be. Smith would finish at -20, and McIlroy, forced to eagle 18, failed to do so and finished in third place. Smith captured his first major championship.

"Disappointed, obviously," McIlroy said. "Yeah, I felt like I didn't do much wrong today, but I didn't do much right either."xxx

Still, it was the first time in Rory McIlroy's career that he had posted top-eight finishes in all four majors that year, including two runner-ups.

At the Tour Championship, McIlroy started the round six shots back of the lead. But just like in past Tour Championships, he put on a ferocious rally and passed Scottie Scheffler and Sungjae Im to win by one shot. It was his third FedEx Cup title since 2016, and with that, he etched himself into the history books by becoming the first player to win the Cup three times. As a result, he won $18 million.

"It's really cool to do something in golf that no one has ever done before," McIlroy told reporters. "Obviously, the history of the FedEx Cup isn't as long as the history of some other tournaments, but to be walking out of here three times a champion, it's very, very satisfying and something that I'm incredibly proud of."[xxxi]

Major championships were still the goal, though, for McIlroy, as was the career grand slam. He went to Augusta in April 2023 for the ninth time with a shot at the career grand slam. He went in with high hopes, with a victory at the CJ Cup, a runner-up at the Arnold Palmer Invitational, and a third place at the World Match Play.

McIlroy shot a 72 after the first round and then made what he said was a colossal mistake—he looked at the leaderboard. He felt pressure when he saw Brooks Koepka getting way out ahead, 10 strokes ahead of him, and he started forcing shots. Next thing you know, Rory was shooting a 77 and missed the cut.

"The worst thing I did that day," McIlroy admitted after his second round 77, "I'm there thinking, 'Jeez, I'm 10 behind already, like I have to start pressing,' when actually what's worked best for me is I can't control what he (Koepka) does, I can't control the leaderboard, and the worst thing I did that day was look at the leaderboard because if I hadn't have known—the winning score ended up being 10-under, I think."[xxxii]

"So, I thought I needed to get to 10-under in the space of like 18 or 27 holes when I actually could have said, 'OK, chill out, it's fine, you know, go and play your normal game, see where you're at.'"[xxxii]

65

But he struggled out of the gate at the Masters and missed the cut. McIlroy then began to question his mental approach going into Augusta National every year. How could he get over that hump?

Disappointed as much as he had ever been, Rory decided to take a short break from golf, putting away the clubs from the end of April until mid-May. He had to put the pressure of winning the Masters behind him and focus on other things.

"It was like, I need to reassess the place I am in my life and what is important to me and what I need to focus my energy on," McIlroy said.[xxxiii]

McIlroy posted three straight top-10s leading into the 2023 U.S. Open, including a T7 at the PGA Championship won by Koepka. McIlroy's drought looked like it might end in Los Angeles after rounds of 65-67 to put him two back of Rickie Fowler after two rounds. After a 69 in the third round, he was just one back of the lead held by Fowler and Wyndham Clark.

Fowler collapsed early in Round 4, leaving just McIlroy and Clark at the top. But just like at the 2022 Open Championship, McIlroy's putter went ice cold. He birdied the first hole but then made par on the next 12. A critical bogey on 14 put him three back of Clark. Despite two late bogeys from Clark, McIlroy still could not find a birdie, and when his birdie putt missed on 18, he came up one shot short and in second place. It was his third runner-up finish and sixth top-10 in his last seven majors.

McIlroy went into the Open Championship with a lot of confidence, having won the Scottish Open the week before. But at Royal Liverpool, the same course he had won the Open Championship on in 2014, he struggled to get anything going. He would post yet another great finish, ending up T6, but well behind the winner Brian Harman, who won by five shots.

Overall, McIlroy's consistency in 2023 almost matched that of Scheffler. He ended the season with 10 straight top-10s to close the year on the PGA Tour. He just could not end his major championship drought.

He started 2024 slowly, which was not a good omen going into Augusta National. His confidence at the Masters seemed to be at an all-time low, trying to put no expectations on himself when he teed off. He made the cut but finished in a distant 22nd place, well back of the winner Scottie Scheffler.

After a T12 at the PGA Championship, McIlroy again found himself with a golden opportunity to win the U.S. Open. He was tied for the lead after the first round and went into the final round in a tie for second, albeit three shots behind leader Bryson DeChambeau.

But McIlroy closed the gap on Sunday, making an early birdie, and finding himself just a shot back of DeChambeau going into the back nine. It was the fourth straight year he went into the back nine of a U.S. Open with a shot to win. The tide then turned at 12. McIlroy, playing a group ahead of DeChambeau, made birdie while DeChambeau followed it up with a bogey. McIlroy was now on top of the leaderboard at -7. It would stay that way when McIlroy went to the par-3 16th hole.

McIlroy hit a fine shot onto the green and nestled his putt to about two feet. Then, shockingly, McIlroy missed the par putt. He was tied for the lead.

On 18, McIlroy found himself short of the green in two, needing a par to at least stay tied with DeChambeau and possibly force a playoff. McIlroy played a fine chip shot that just went past the hole by about three feet. But it was a slick putt down the hill with some break. McIlroy tapped his par putt but did not play enough break. The putt hit the lip and went by. It was another short miss for McIlroy. He now trailed by one as DeChambeau sat off the fairway in trouble on 18.

DeChambeau could not get much on his second shot and put it about 30 yards short of the green in the bunker. From there, he played a great bunker shot to about four feet short of the hole. DeChambeau then went on to sink the par putt as television cameras showed a dejected McIlroy leave Pinehurst in disgust. It was a horrible way to lose a tournament.

McIlroy seemed to lose a lot of energy after that loss. He went to the Open Championship at Royal Troon and missed the cut. He competed well in the Olympics in Paris but just missed out on a medal. He finished the year at No. 3 in the world, behind both Scottie Scheffler and Xander Schauffele. While 2024 was a solid year, that U.S. Open loss haunted him.

LIV-PGA Feud

When players like Phil Mickelson, Dustin Johnson, Louis Oosthuizen, Bryson DeChambeau, and others left for Saudi Arabia's LIV Tour, an alternative to the PGA Tour, no one was more vocal about it than Rory McIlroy. A staunch advocate of the PGA Tour, McIlroy was not shy about voicing his opinion against those who joined LIV.

It had started in 2022 when Greg Norman, LIV's CEO, hosted an event in London for all those interested. The new tour, led by Norman, threw millions of dollars at golfers to play in a more relaxed format and schedule with just 54 holes compared to the PGA Tour's 72 holes. From the get-go, McIlroy voiced his disapproval of it.

"It's a shame that it's going to fracture the game," McIlroy said. "The professional game is the window shop into golf. If the general public are confused about who is playing where and what tournament's on this week and who is, you know, oh, he plays there, OK, and he doesn't get into these events. It just becomes so confusing."[xxxiv]

Of course, Rory was not wrong. The new tour indeed drove a massive wedge into the game. PGA Tour commissioner Jay Monahan suspended players who jumped over, not allowing them back onto the PGA Tour. Over time, prominent players took millions of dollars to jump to LIV–names like Jon Rahm, Brooks Koepka, Cameron Smith, and Tyrell Hatton. By 2023, the two tours were at odds, and the PGA Tour was actively seeking ways to make their Tour more enticing so players would not leave.

"There's no room in the golf world for LIV Golf. I don't agree with what LIV is doing. If LIV went away tomorrow, I'd be super happy. My stance hasn't softened on that," McIlroy said. "My stance on where the money is coming from is where I've sort of softened. If these guys are willing to do that and scrap the whole LIV thing, that would be ideal."[xxxiv]

McIlroy's relationship with several players was strained because of the drama, including Phil Mickelson and Sergio Garcia. Things got truly ugly for a while, but eventually, the frameworks of a merger were announced in which LIV and the PGA Tour would begin working toward a solution. However, as of the summer of 2025, negotiations continue on how to bring the two tours together.

McIlroy's stance against LIV has since softened a bit, however, and his frustration with the PGA Tour at times has grown, as they have been unable to work out a deal. McIlroy even resigned from the board in charge of trying to work out a deal.

"I just think I've got a lot going on in my life between my golf game, my family, and my growing investment portfolio, my involvement in TGL, and I just felt like something had to give," McIlroy said. "I just didn't feel like I could commit the time and the energy into doing that."[xxxiv]

McIlroy has now accepted LIV and has made amends with many of the players over there. He even agreed that players on the Tour should be allowed to be selected for the Ryder Cup teams. Rumors at one point even blew up that McIlroy was open to joining the Tour, but he immediately shot those down as pure fiction.

2025 Masters

Rory McIlroy's confidence going into the Masters could not be any bigger. If this was not the year, one had to wonder if it would ever happen—after all, he was now 35 years old. It was a dream start to the season for him. He started it by winning a premier event at the AT&T Pebble Beach Pro-Am. Then, he came from behind at the Players Championship, forcing a playoff against J.J. Spaun and winning it on a Monday morning. It was his second Players title and second big victory of the season against an elite field.

There was also the fact that Scottie Scheffler had not gotten off to a great start to the season, opening the door for McIlroy to take him down at the Masters.

But after the first round, it looked like it would be another letdown week for McIlroy at Augusta National. After a hot start to the round, he came to 15 and knocked a chip shot past the hole and into the water. The triple bogey ruined what was a promising round. McIlroy finished at even, seven shots back of leader Justin Rose, who went out and shot a 65.

It is important to note that two years ago, McIlroy was in a similar position and felt like he had to make a move on Friday. He forced things, shot 77 in the second round, and missed the cut. But McIlroy had learned from his mistakes, played more relaxed on Friday, and chipped away at the leader. Rose got out to -10 but came back to the field and finished -8. McIlroy just kept plodding along, slowly making birdies and cruising to a 66, putting himself at -6 and two shots back of the lead.

With momentum on his side, McIlroy got out to a blistering and historic start on Saturday. He opened the third round with six 3s, the first-ever player to do that. That start included going birdie-eagle-birdie-par-birdie-par to start his round, -5 through five holes. As a result, he bolted out to the lead and at one point looked like he might destroy the field, having opened up a 3-shot lead. But then he cooled down and even backed up some, having made a 6 on the par-5 8th hole, allowing players like DeChambeau and Corey Conners to inch closer to the lead.

However, McIlroy would not be deposed; he got key birdies at 13 and 15 and would close at -12, two shots ahead of DeChambeau and four shots ahead of Conners. It seemed like it was his Masters to lose now. The thrilling pairing of McIlroy and DeChambeau caught a lot of attention, given their back-nine battle at the 2024 U.S. Open. The two also were not exactly considered the best of friends, and things were pretty quiet as they walked the course together on Sunday.

McIlroy got off to a slow start on Sunday in search of the career grand slam. He double-bogeyed the first hole, and in the snap of a finger, his two-shot lead was gone. After DeChambeau birdied the second hole and McIlroy parred, he was now trailing by one.

But McIlroy settled down. After DeChambeau found trouble at 3 and made bogey, McIlroy chipped a beautiful second to within a few feet and sank the birdie to go one ahead again.

Then there was another two-shot swing on the fourth when McIlroy made a birdie and DeChambeau bogeyed. Just like that, McIlroy was three ahead.

McIlroy was in cruise control from there. He stuck his approaches close at 9 and 10 and made a birdie to go to -14, extending his lead to five shots. After DeChambeau put his second shot in the water on 11, he was basically out of the picture.

On the par-5 13th hole, McIlroy, at -13 now, played it safe and laid up. As he prepared to play his third shot from under 100 yards, his lead was three over Rose. But then, in what was perhaps the most shocking shot of the tournament, McIlroy muffed his fourth shot and it went into the creek. Was he crumbling under pressure? He double-bogeyed, and his lead was just one. Then, Rose birdied 16, and it was tied.

McIlroy was now seemingly falling apart and bogeyed 14 to fall out of the lead. But on the par-5 15th, just as Justin Rose made a bogey on 17, McIlroy hit the shot of the tournament, a sweeping four-iron that drew perfectly around the trees, landed just onto the green, and stopped within several feet of the cup. Although he missed the eagle putt, he tapped in for a birdie and was back in the lead. He would hold that lead as he sat in the fairway on 18, one ahead of Rose and the career grand slam in sight.

But again, McIlroy made a shocking mistake. He blocked his shot right, and it went into the bunker. He nestled it up to about 10 feet but missed the par putt that would have given him the win Masters. Now, he and Rose were going to a playoff.

The weight was all on McIlroy's shoulders now. If he blew this opportunity, he had to wonder if he could ever recover. After Rose put his shot some 20 feet from the hole, McIlroy stepped up and hit it about 15 feet past the hole. However, the green had slope to it from back to front, and combined with the spin, the ball funneled back to the hole. It just kept getting closer and closer until it stopped within a couple of feet of the hole. What a shot!

After Rose missed his birdie putt, McIlroy stepped up to his ball with a shot to win the Masters. This time, he knocked it into the center of the cup. At that point, absolute relief and joy overcame Rory as he fell to the ground and began weeping, his hands and arms over his face.

"I would say it was 14 years in the making, from going out with a four-shot lead in 2011, feeling like I could have gotten it done there," McIlroy said. "Yeah, there was a lot of pent-up emotion that just came out on that 18th green. A moment like that makes all the years and all the close calls worth it."[xxxv]

The emotions just came pouring out of him. All that hard work to win the Masters and accomplish the Grand Slam—he had finally done it! It was a rollercoaster ride unlike any he'd ever been on, but he did it. The momentous win made Rory McIlroy only the seventh player in golf history to win the career grand slam.

"This is my 17th time here, and I started to wonder if it would ever be my time," McIlroy said. "I think the last 10 years coming here with the burden of the grand slam on my shoulders and trying to achieve that, yeah, I'm sort of wondering what we're all going to talk about going into next year's Masters."xxxv

In the green jacket ceremony, McIlroy was very emotional and nearly broke down in tears again as he thanked his mom and dad watching at home in Northern Ireland. It was one of the most iconic moments in Masters history.

"Welcome to the club @McIlroyRory," Tiger Woods posted on X, one of those seven career grand slam winners. "Completing the grand slam at Augusta is something special. Your determination during this round, and this entire journey has shown through, and now you're a part of history. Proud of you!"

As might be expected when you win something of that magnitude, McIlroy lost a little motivation following the victory. Frankly, it seems to have taken a lot out of him. He struggled to make the cut at the PGA Championship and U.S. Open, finishing well back of the eventual winners, Scottie Scheffler and J.J. Spaun, respectively. At the Open Championship in July 2025, marking his return to Royal Portrush in Northern Ireland, he finished tied for seventh place.

But in September, McIlroy won the Amgen Irish Open at the K Club, putting up a brilliant performance that featured a sudden-death playoff against Joakim Lagergren. Undoubtedly, there will be many more thrilling moments to come.

Chapter 5: Personal Life

Much like Tiger Woods, when you're Rory McIlroy and in the public eye as much as he is, your dating life is always a hot topic. There's no escaping it. McIlroy first experienced this when he dated famous tennis player Caroline Wozniacki.

The two were rumored to have started dating around the time that McIlroy won the U.S. Open in 2011. Everywhere they went, there were cameras on them since they were both superstars in their respective sports. Two years later, on New Year's Eve 2013, McIlroy proposed to Wozniacki, and she accepted. But just went everything seemed to be going great and wedding bells were not far off, the two broke up. McIlroy took full responsibility for breaking off the engagement.

"The problem is mine," McIlroy said. "The wedding invitations issued at the weekend made me realize that I wasn't ready for all that marriage entails. I wish Caroline all the happiness she deserves and thank her for the great times we've had."[xxxvi]

Not long after McIlroy and Wozniacki broke up, he became involved with Erica Stoll, who worked for the PGA of America as a transport official. McIlroy first met Stoll in 2012 when he was trying to get a ride to the Ryder Cup. They dated for a long time until finally getting engaged in 2015. Two years ago, they had a dream wedding at Ashford Castle on the west coast of Ireland overlooking the spectacularly picturesque Lough Corrib.

On August 31, 2020, Rory and Erica had their first child together, a girl they called Poppy. But sadly, their marriage has not been smooth sailing. In 2024, Rory filed for divorce and was even rumored to be seeing CBS golf personality Amanda Balionis. However, they were able to repair their issues, and Rory canceled the paperwork for the divorce. As of the summer of 2025, they are back living a happy life together with Poppy.

McIlroy has kept busy even when off the golf course, devoting time to philanthropy and business opportunities. His partnership with Tiger Woods on the new TGL League has been a great success thus far. The league uses indoor golf technology and simulators for team competitions, creating a strong alternative to the LIV Tour's team format. Golfers hit their shots into a big screen, which then transforms into a video game-like golf course, showing where the shot went. The league aired in primetime on ESPN between January and March.

"Tiger and I have been a part of this from day one, and whenever you see the concepts and the renderings, you think, 'Yeah, that looks really cool,'" McIlroy said. "But until you actually stand in here (the SoFi Center) and you see what they've been able to do, I think the scale of it is the thing for me that blows my mind. Every time I step in here, I'm just blown away by the size of the screen, the fact that we're able to put something that looks like golf on a stage like this. It's really cool, and we're obviously really excited about it within the game of golf. I think a lot of other people outside of the game are going to see this and hopefully get excited about it as well."[xxxvii]

Many of McIlroy's ventures are operated by his business manager Sean O'Flaherty. He recently partnered with a few investment funds, including Symphony Ventures and TPG Sports. Much of McIlroy's winnings are put into these investment funds, which grow over time and acquire different companies.

McIlroy's empire has grown steadily thanks to his savvy business sense. He owns shares in various platforms, including Golf Genius, TickPick, Troon Golf, TMIW Sports, Golf+, Puttery, Golf Pass, Kin Insurance, Alpine (Formula One), and Kaia Health. All these business interests have helped to skyrocket McIlroy's net worth, which is estimated to be around $250 million, with $100 million in career earnings. In 2024 alone, McIlroy made $45 million off the golf course, according to *Forbes*. He also has endorsement deals with Nike, Omega, and TaylorMade. His Nike contract is reported to be around $100 million.[xxxviii]

But another big piece of Rory's off-course life is spent in the gym. Not many people realize just how much golfers exercise and lift weights, and McIlroy is one of the most active. He spent a lot of time early in his career with physiologist Dr. Stephen McGregor, transforming his body from a pudgy youth to a lean and athletic-looking athlete who hits the ball as far as anyone on Tour.

Early in his career, McIlroy actually took some heat for his heavy lifting. Many attributed Tiger Woods' injuries and quick decline in his

30s due to weights. But McIlroy snapped back at the criticism, citing that it was part of his plan to get better in golf.

"I'm a golfer, not a weightlifter," McIlroy said.[i]

Rory's non-tournament schedule includes waking up at 5:30 a.m., eating a light breakfast, and then being at the gym by 6:30 a.m. for a one-hour cardio workout. He then eats another breakfast before hitting the golf course for five-plus hours of practice with a lunch in between. When that's finished, he heads back to the weight room for a bigger workout, working more on muscular exercises. By the time he's done and eating dinner, it's well after 6 p.m. In other words, to be great, he puts a lot of work in.[i]

"Going to the gym is great for your body, but it's also great for your mind," McIlroy said.[xxxix]

But Rory does find time for other things, especially philanthropy in the offseason. He works with the Rory Foundation, an organization that works with several children's charities and provides them with opportunities to do activities they normally could not afford.

"When I was younger, my parents sacrificed everything to allow me to play the game I love," McIlroy said. "Having that support from my family gave me the opportunity to chase my dreams. But I know that every child is not so fortunate. My aim is that The Rory Foundation will support children's charities big and small, around the world, that try to give kids that helping hand."[i]

One of the biggest charities closest to McIlroy's heart is the UK-based Royal Mencap Society. He's donated much of his prize money over the years to the organization that houses and aids children with learning disabilities. Additionally, Rory has spent a lot of time with these children, who are dear to his heart.

In 2011, McIlroy was named a UNICEF Goodwill Ambassador and made a trip to Haiti to visit the children and families whose homes were ravaged by a deadly earthquake. It was the first of multiple visits he made to the region. He actually won the U.S. Open shortly after his first visit there.

"Pretty emotional day today. Great to see all the work UNICEF do to help and educate kids in this grief-stricken country," McIlroy said.[i]

McIlroy called the trip an eye-opening experience. He enjoyed having the opportunity to do all he could to help the children there and donated money in an effort to make a positive difference.

"The chance that these children are getting to be kids and enjoy themselves is so important for their well-being," McIlroy said. "Being here at this child-friendly space gives them the chance to play with their friends and enjoy themselves—helping them escape for a little while every day from the difficult situations they are growing up in."[xl]

In a profession known for some bristly personalities, McIlroy is one of the more liked guys in the game. He maintains a strong friendship on and off the course with Irishman Shane Lowry. The two regularly hang out together and even team up in competitions.

McIlroy loves to travel all around the world and reportedly has three mansions and two apartments. His main home for years was in Jupiter, Florida, where he owned a 13,000-square-foot estate. He has another mansion in La Quinta, California, and a third home in Northern Ireland. His two apartments are said to be in New York City and the United Arab Emirates.[xli] Of course, he bought a beautiful new home for his parents in Holywood around 2009, shortly after establishing himself as a professional. And just recently, Rory sold the home in Jupiter and built a stunning new mansion in Wentworth, England, where the family moved over the summer. Not bad for a boy who rose to fame from hard-working, middle-class origins!

Chapter 6: Legacy

Rory McIlroy could retire today and be instantly inducted into the World Golf Hall of Fame. So, it is not a question of if but *when*. His resume includes 48 worldwide wins, 5 grand slam titles, 8 Ryder Cups, 3 FedEx Cups (the most of anyone), 2 Players Championships, 7 Players of the Year Awards (3 PGA and 4 DP World Tour), 6 Race to Dubai titles, and 3 World Golf Championships.

McIlroy is already one of just seven legendary players to have won the career grand slam and is tied for 17th all-time for most PGA Tour wins with 29. Obviously, he will further climb up that list before he retires. He needs just 16 more wins to catch Phil Mickelson, who is eighth on the list and fourth in most victories since 1960.[iii]

McIlroy has five major championships, making him one of the most decorated European golfers of all time. Among modern-day golfers, Nick Faldo owns the most majors of any European player with six, while Seve Ballesteros has five.

McIlroy also ranks 12th all-time for most European/DP World Tour wins with 19. However, most of the players above him played many more tournaments on the Tour than he did, since Rory spent a lot of time playing on the PGA Tour since 2010. His six Race to Dubai titles, an honor given to the top points leader on the DP World Tour, are just two shy of the record eight held by Colin Montgomerie.

One record McIlroy seems destined to break is the most European Ryder Cup appearances. The 2025 rendition will be his eighth consecutive. He needs three more Ryder Cups to catch Nick Faldo, who has 11 appearances. Phil Mickelson holds the most for both sides with 12. McIlroy also has 16 match wins, 9 short of Sergio Garcia's record of 25. There are also rumors that McIlroy could captain the 2027 Ryder Cup in Ireland, while Tiger Woods may captain the U.S. squad. But as of now, those are just rumors.

As exceptional as he is, Rory McIlroy's quest to become the greatest golfer of all time will likely come up somewhat short. He is just too far behind Tiger Woods and Jack Nicklaus in terms of major wins and overall Tour victories. But being the greatest of the post-Tiger era is an honor he would like to have. That puts him in competition with players like Scottie Scheffler and Brooks Koepka. In terms of major titles, Koepka is the only one who has been able to match McIlroy. However, Koepka does not have the career grand slam, nor does he have nearly as many PGA Tour wins as McIlroy.

Many see Scheffler as McIlroy's biggest rival and the player who could possibly have the better career when all is said and done. McIlroy is seven years older, so his numbers are more impressive at the moment. McIlroy has 5 majors to Scheffler's 3, and 29 PGA Tour wins to Scheffler's 16.

But does Scheffler have the longevity to keep it going? Many players, like Jordan Spieth and Dustin Johnson, have had great starts to their careers but failed to keep it going for a long stretch of time. What makes McIlroy's career particularly impressive is that he has been at the top of his game now for roughly 15 years. That's hard to do in today's day and age. When you think of golfers who have been able to play great in their 20s, 30s, and 40s, only a few names come to mind, such as Jack Nicklaus, Phil Mickelson, and Gary Player. Not even Tiger Woods saw much success in his 40s. It's unclear if McIlroy will stay relevant in his 40s, but thus far, he has shown the ability to play great for a long period of time.

The biggest question surrounding McIlroy, however, will likely be his motivation. McIlroy stated before the 2025 U.S. Open that winning the Masters was a great release of pressure, and he seemed to have lost some inner drive after that. Does he want to be remembered as one of the greatest of all time? Or was winning the career grand slam the pinnacle of his dreams? Perhaps not even Rory himself knows.

"You have this event in your life that you've worked towards, and it happens, sometimes it's hard to find the motivation to get back on the horse and go again," McIlroy said.[xlii]

McIlroy said he never had dreams beyond winning the grand slam. He does not know his goals at the moment and will have to reset them after finally winning the Masters. Thus, he does not really have a plan. However, he did say that he knows that drive will come back—and of that, we have no doubt.

Conclusion

Rory McIlroy's 2025 Masters win has elevated him into that special category of professional golfers that we call a legend. Eventually, he will join the Hall of Fame and forever be remembered as one of the select few players to ever achieve the career grand slam.

McIlroy's dream was ultimately made possible because of the love and support of his parents, and as illustrated in this story, he is extremely grateful for the sacrifices they made for him. But it was not just them alone; McIlroy also worked incredibly hard to become the player he is today. He was up at sunrise and working until sunset to be an elite golfer. He knew the hard work and dedication that went into being a professional golfer and put everything he had into it.

"To be a top-class athlete, you have to train hard, you have to eat right, you have to get enough rest. The way golf is going nowadays, you have to treat yourself as an athlete."[xxxix]

But what makes the success story of Rory McIlroy even more enthralling is that he had all the pressure in the world on his shoulders, and he not only met those expectations but also went beyond them. As a young boy, he was called the next "Tiger Woods." That's an incredibly hard label to put on a child. So many others have stumbled under the weight of heavy expectations and not been able to handle the pressure. But McIlroy's motivation and love for the game allowed him to achieve his dreams and prove everyone right who said that he would one day be one of the greatest golfers of all time.

Rory McIlroy has demonstrated what it really takes to be great at golf. It is not just about spending a few hours on the golf course every day and expecting to be a PGA Tour player. It takes hours upon hours of hard work on the course and in the gym, along with eating right and keeping a strong mental game in place. It is about never losing your focus and dedication, even in the most daunting of moments. Setbacks happen, but it is how you respond to them that ultimately defines you. He certainly faced his fair share of setbacks and disappointments, but one could argue that nobody has bounced back from failure better than Rory McIlroy.

Final Word/About the Author

Wow! You made it to the end of this book, and you're reading the About the Author section? Now that's impressive and puts you in the top 1% of readers.

Since you're curious about me, I was born and raised in Norwalk, Connecticut. Growing up, I could often be found spending many nights watching basketball, soccer, and football matches with my father in the family living room. I love sports and everything that sports can embody. I believe that sports are one of the most genuine forms of competition, heart, and determination. I write my works to learn more about influential athletes in the hopes that from my writing, you the reader can walk away inspired to put in an equal if not greater amount of hard work and perseverance to pursue your goals.

I've written these stories for over a decade, and loved every moment of it. When I look back on my life, I am most proud of not just having covered so many different athletes' inspirational stories, but for all the times I got e-mails or handwritten letters from readers on the impact my books have had on them.

So thank you from the bottom of my heart for allowing me to do work I find meaningful. I am incredibly grateful for you and your support.

If you're new to my sports biography books, welcome. I have goodies for you as a thank you from me in the pages ahead.

Before we get there though, I have a question for you...

Were you inspired at any point in this book?

If so, would you help someone else get inspired too?

You see, my mission is to inspire sports fans of all ages around the world that anything is possible through hard work and perseverance...but the only way to accomplish this mission is by reaching everyone.

So here's my ask from you:

Most people, regardless of what the saying tells them to do, judge a book by its cover (and its reviews).

If you enjoyed *Rory McIlroy: The Inspiring Story of One of Golf's Fearless Champions,* please help inspire another person needing to hear this story by leaving a review.

Doing so takes less than a minute, and that dose of inspiration can change another person's life in more ways than you can even imagine.

To get that generous 'feel good' feeling and help another person, all you have to do is take 60 seconds and leave a review.

If you're on Audible: hit the three dots in the top right of your device, click rate & review, then leave a few sentences about the book with a star rating.

If you're reading on Kindle or an e-reader: scroll to the bottom of the book, then swipe up and it will prompt a review for you.

If for some reason these have changed: you can head back to Amazon and leave a review right on the book's page.

Thank you for helping another person, and for your support of my writing as an independent author.

Clayton

Like what you read?
Then you'll love these too!

This book is one of hundreds of stories I've written. If you enjoyed this story on Rory McIlroy, you'll love my other sports biography book series too.

You can find them by visiting my website at claytongeoffreys.com or by scanning the QR code below to follow my author page on Amazon.

Here's a little teaser about each of my sports biography book series:

Basketball Biography Books: This series covers the stories of over 100 NBA greats such as Stephen Curry, LeBron James, Michael Jordan, and more.

Football Biography Books: This series covers the stories of over 50 NFL greats such as Peyton Manning, Tom Brady, and Patrick Mahomes, and more.

Baseball Biography Books: This series covers the stories of over 40 MLB greats such as Aaron Judge, Shohei Ohtani, Mike Trout, and more.

Basketball Leadership Biography Books: This series covers the stories of basketball coaching greats such as Steve Kerr, Gregg Popovich, John Wooden, and more.

Soccer Biography Books: This series covers the stories of tennis greats such as Neymar, Harry Kane, Robert Lewandowski, and more.

Tennis Biography Books: This series covers the stories of tennis greats such as Serena Williams, Rafael Nadal, Andy Roddick, and more.

Women's Basketball Biography Books: This series covers the stories of many WNBA greats such as Diana Taurasi, Sue Bird, Sabrina Ionescu, and more.

Lastly, if you'd like to join my exclusive list where I let you know about my latest books, and thank you for your purchase, go to **claytongeoffreys.com/goodies**.

Or, if you don't like typing, scan the following QR code here to go there directly. See you there!

Clayton

References

[i] Beattie, Jillie. "The Story of Rory." *McIlroy.Belfastlive.co.uk.* Accessed Aug 2025, Web.

[ii] @classicgolfclips. "Rory's Major Debut." *YouTube.* Accessed Aug 2025, Web.

[iii] "Rory McIlroy." *PGATour.com.* Accessed Aug 2025, Web.

[iv] "Official World Golf Ranking." *Owgr.com.* Accessed Aug 2025, Web.

[v] Caruso, Skyler. "All About Rory's Parents, Rosie and Gerry." *Yahoosports.com.* 12 Jun 2024, Web.

[vi] Dethier, Dylan. "Rory McIlroy's Childhood Coach Has 1 Piece of Advice for Every Golf Parent." *Golf.com.* 23 Jun 2020, Web.

[vii] Kerr-Dineen, Luke. "Rory McIlroy: This is My Best Advice for Junior Golfers." *Golf.com.* 31 May 2022, Web.

[viii] Simpson, Mark. "Former Principal Says He Took 'Risk' Over McIlroy's Absences." *BBC.com.* 17 Apr 2025, Web.

[ix] Martin, Sean. "Inside McIlroy's 61 at Royal Portrush at Age 16." *PGATour.com.* 16 Jul 2019, Web.

[x] "Hollywood Pride: The Amateur Career of Rory McIlroy." *GolfMonthly.com.* 14 Jul 2021, Web.

[xi] Murray, Ewan. "How a Young Rory McIlroy Burst Onto the Open Scene in 2007." *TheGuardian.com.* 17 Jul 2017, Web.

[xii] Rapaport, Dan. "Rory McIlroy Remembers an All-Time Meltdown as a Teenage Rookie." *GolfDigest.com.* Accessed Aug 2025, Web.

[xiii] "McIlroy Gets Maiden Victory." *GolfDigest.com.* 31 Jan 2009, Web.

[xiv] Cannizzaro, Mark. "Rory McIlroy's Surprising Revelation About His First PGA Tour Win at Quail Hollow." *NYPost.com.* 4 May 2025, Web.

[xv] Tait, Camila. "How Rory McIlroy Stormed Onto the World State at Quail Hollow in 2010." *SkySports.com.* 6 May 2016, Web.

[xvi] Mitchell, Kevin. "The Open 2010: Rory McIlroy Still Has Faith After Grim Survival Fight." *TheGuardian.com.* 16 Jul 2010, Web.

[xvii] Bantock, Jack. "The Haunting Masters That Changed Rory McIlroy's Career." *CNN.com.* 9 Apr 2024, Web.

[xviii] "Rory McIlroy Runs Away With U.S. Open Title." *ESPN.com.* 19 Jun 2011, Web.

[xix] "Rory McIlroy Wins Honda Classic, Takes Over as No. 1 Golfer in the World." *Jacksonville.com.* Accessed Aug 2025, Web.

[xx] Paisley, Kent. "Kiawah 10 Years Later: A Record-Breaking Anniversary for Rory McIlroy." *PGAChampionship.com.* 12 Aug 2022, Web.

xxi Kerr-Dineen, Luke. "How One Word Won Rory McIlroy the 2014 British Open." *GolfDigest.com.* 14 Jul 2023, Web.

xxii Woodard, Adam. "Man on Fire: Rory McIlroy at Valhalla." *PGAChampionship.com.* 15 May 2024, Web.

xxiii "Rory Wins PGA Tour Player of the Year; Hadley Named Top Rookie." *PGA.com.* 1 Oct 2014, Web.

xxiv "McIlroy's Third Win of Day Earns WGC-Cadillac Match Play Title." *TheGuardian.com.* 3 May 2015, Web.

xxv Murray, Ewan. "Rory McIlroy Wins DP Tour World Championship and Race to Dubai." *TheGuardian.com.* 22 Nov 2015, Web.

xxvi "Tour Championship: Rory McIlroy Wins Title in Atlanta To Claim FedEx Cup." *BBC.com.* 26 Sep 2016, Web.

xxvii "Flashback: Rory McIlroy Ends Victory Drought With 2018 Arnold Palmer Invitational Win." *SkySports.com.* 5 Mar 2019, Web.

xxviii "Rory McIlroy Wins the Players Championship in Dramatic Fashion." *PGATour.com.* 2019, Web.

xxix Beall, Joel. "In an Upset, Rory McIlroy Wins PGA Tour Player of the Year Over Brooks Koepka." *GolfDigest.com.* 11 Sep 2019, Web.

xxx Beall, Joel. "Rory McIlroy Didn't Win the Claret Jug. But he Won This Open." *GolfDigest.com.* 17 Jul 2022, Web.

xxxi Bantock, Jack. "Tour Championship: Rory McIlroy Overturns Six-Shot Deficit at FedEx Cup to Make Tour Championship History." *CNN.com.* 29 Aug 2022, Web.

xxxii Piastowski, Nick. "'The Worst Thing I Did': Rory McIlroy Reveals a Mistake He Made at 2023 Masters." *Golf.com.* 9 Jan 2024, Web.

xxxiii "McIlroy Needed a 'Reset' After Missing Cut at Masters." *APNews.com.* 2 May 2023, Web.

xxxiv Ryan, Shane. "Rory McIlroy's Evolving Stance on LIV Golf and the PIF: A Comprehensive Timeline." *GolfDigest.com.* 9 Feb 2024, Web.

xxxv Schlabach, Mark. "Rory McIlroy Wins Masters in Playoff to Earn Career Grand Slam." *ESPN.com.* 13 Apr 2025, Web.

xxxvi Hudgins, Ryan. "Rory McIlroy and Caroline Wozniacki's Relationship Timeline." *USWeekly.com.* 16 Apr 2025, Web.

xxxvii Morse, Ben. "It's Golf, But It's Reimagined." *CNN.com.* 25 Jan 2025, Web.

xxxviii Srinivisan, Hiranmayi. "Rory McIlroy's 9-Figure Net Worth–How He Made Millions On and Off the Golf Course." *Investopedia.com.* 19 Apr 2025, Web.

xxxix "Rory McIlroy Quotes." *BrainyQuote.com.* Accessed Aug 2025, Web.

[xl] Busbee, Jay. "Rory McIlroy's Haitian Expedition Opens His Eyes." *YahooSports.com.* 9 Jun 2011, Web.

[xli] Chauhan, Jutin. "Rory McIlroy's Luxurious Lifestyle: All About the Houses He Owns Around the World." *EssentiallySports.com.* 29 Sep 2024, Web.

[xlii] Harig, Bob. "After His Masters Triumph, Rory McIlroy Is Struggling to Recharge His Mind and His Game. *SI.com.* 9 Jun 2025, Web.

Printed in Dunstable, United Kingdom